FISHING JOURNAL

*A diary designed especially for the ease
and benefit of the serious fly angler*

Mark Koenig
&
Paul Petersen

Frank Amato

PORTLAND

FISHING JOURNAL

*A diary designed especially for the ease
and benefit of the serious fly angler*

Written and Designed
by Mark Koenig and Paul Petersen
Illustrations: Richard Bunse
Cover photograph: Jim Schollmeyer
Back cover photograph: Dave Hughes

10 9 8 7 6 5 4 3 2

CONTENTS

ABOUT THE AUTHORS

Mark Koenig is a recent graduate from Oregon State University where he earned a B.S. in fisheries science. He is a self confessed fly fishing addict, and admits to spending too much of his time practicing and enjoying the sport. His degree in fisheries science is the result of his ongoing quest to better understand water, the creatures who live in it, and the subtle interactions that make aquatic ecosystems tick. Mark presently lives in Ashland where he works on a variety of projects which help support his habit.

Paul Petersen was born in the small town of Trail and attended Southern Oregon State University. Paul's passion for fly fishing and devotion to conservation have involved him in almost every aspect of the sport. He has been active as a guide for many years, working all over the state with a special emphasis on Oregon's spring creeks. He's been in the retail side of the sport since the early seventies, and had the pleasure of owning and operating a fly fishing resort and shop on the Metolius for much of the eighties. Having instructed courses on the art and science of the sport for much of his life, he's now helped over 800 adult learners discover the sport, including an official political delegation from the former U.S.S.R.. Paul's adventures have brought him back to the Rogue Valley, where he continues guiding, teaching, and now manages Mckenzie Outfitter's fly shop in Medford.

FORWARD

Many years ago I chanced upon a true master of the sport while fishing on the Metolius River. I stood on the bank and watched as he patiently worked the water with a grace and skill that was poetic to the eye. He moved in a slow deliberate manner, carefully noticing all that was taking place around him and reacting to each situation as if it had been expected. With more then a little envy I watched as he took several fish from water which had been barren to me. Then he did an odd thing. He stopped fishing, pulled out a note card on which he scribbled a few lines, then as quickly as he had stopped resumed fishing.

This was my first exposure to the practice of keeping stream notes and the beginning of a long friendship with a true gentlemen of the river, Mr Harold Beach. Since that first encounter I've enjoyed many wonderful days on the river with Harold, to whom I owe much for the many things he has taught me. Most important of all, Harold taught me that we are all students of the water and that our personal development and success as a fly fishermen depends greatly upon how actively we embrace this role. Harold was and is a superb student, devoting as much time to observation and thought as he does to actually fishing. Not surprisingly, his success and enjoyment of the sport reflects this devotion.

As for myself, I challenged to pursue this philosophy in my own fishing, and have for many years kept my own notes as a student of the water. With a love for the out-of-doors I've enjoyed many years working as mountain and river guide, owned and operated fly shops, and have had the pleasure of instructing others in the art and science of the sport. It is only after spending so many years totally involved in the sport that I have come to realize the total importance of having recorded my experiences and observations. These written records have been invaluable to me, both in my personal development as a fly fishermen and in my professional career within the sport. From experience and observation comes theory. From theory comes strategy and technique, and from these come the joy of increased ability and success. Keeping notes has greatly aided me in this process of learning, and I believe it is the only way to take full advantage of the lessons to be had when on the water.

Over the years I've used almost everything imaginable for keeping my own records; index cards, blank books, even the occasional piece of scratch paper. With the completion of this journal I've finally got something I can use and be satisfied with. Having helped in its creation, I know it meets my own demanding needs and feel it will be of great benefit to other student anglers as well. As I continue my own exploration, I challenge each of you to explore the water in your life and its many mysteries. Perhaps this journal and the platform it provides will encourage you to take up the challenge and use the information you record to better understand the rivers and hatches that you fish. The old man river, Mr. Harold Beach showed me the importance and ways of being a good student of the water. I hope the journal provides you with the same help and guidance he so graciously gave to me, and that you too realize the benefits to be gained as fellow student of the water.

Paul Dean Petersen
Ashland, Oregon

INTRODUCTION

The reasons for keeping a fishing journal are many. It serves as a diary as well as a data book, a platform on which experiences and observations are remembered and from which new connections and ideas are formed. It is the key to understanding local hatches, or simply a way to remember how to get there and what you should bring. It can act as a record of your catch, or a place to jot down the tying instructions for a great new pattern of which you were loaned only one. It is what you make it: a chronicle of yourself and your adventures, and a tool which allows you to better use these experiences to enhance your future endeavors.

Many feel it would be too much trouble to keep a journal, but they are greatly mistaken. Our understanding and ability as fly fishermen is a culmination of our experiences, and more precisely what we have been able to learn from them. A journal provides such an advantage in this learning process, that the benefits gained by the angler who keeps one far out weigh the few moments lost in its maintenance. For those of us who have incorporated a journal into our collection of gear, there is no question that it has earned its place as an important component of our angling

5

FISHING JOURNAL

success and enjoyment.

I started working on this journal because I wanted something that would better meet my needs. I had looked around at what was available and found that the journals were either too inflexible for me, or simply blank pages with no organization at all.

I wanted a format in which information could be organized and recorded quickly in a standardized fashion, while retaining the ability to accommodate additional detail when wanted as well as observations or thoughts that were unique to a particular outing. Also, I wanted more then just a good format for recording information, I wanted a framework which aided in the translation of numerous observations into cohesive chunks of knowledge. Lastly, I wanted it to be a convenient size for carrying in a vest, but not so small that its functionality was limited or that it was difficult to use.

The journal before you is the product of these desires, the combined efforts of Paul and myself to create a document that fulfilled these desires, and a long line of thoughts, re-thoughts and revisions. We hope the end result of our efforts serve you well, and welcome any questions or comments you might have.

The appendix (USING THE JOURNAL) provides explanations and examples of the components in the journal and lays out some of the ways in which they can be used. A great many things can be done with the information you collect, and each of you will explore these as you see fit. We hope the platform provided helps you to this end, and that you enjoy its use and the pleasures of increased success and understanding it can bring.

IDENTIFYING AQUATIC INSECTS

Identifying aquatic insects is an important skill to the angler who wishes to better understand and match the hatches he or she often fishes. Each angler decides how far to develop this skill and what level of insect identification is convienent and functional in meeting their needs. Generally, it is most practical for the angler to work at the level of Family and Genus. Species within these groups typically share similar enough habitats, physical characteristics, and behavioral traits to be grouped together and still provide excellent and accurrate information for angling purposes. There are exceptions, and I encourage you to be as specific in your studies as your time, experience and desire allows. Whether you dwelve a little or a lot into the world of aquatic entomology, There's no question that your efforts will be rewarded,

This section describes the basic characteristics of the major orders of aquatic insects, but to make more specific identifications you'll need to refer to texts which deal specifically with aquatic insects. There are a great number of books on the subject, and you should explore what is available. I would reccommend two books, which cover most everything needed by the angler/ameture aquatic entomologist. Additional works are required to key insects to species, but these two books make a great foundation for the treatment of aquatic insects and have all the references you'll need to get more information if desired.

The Complete Book Of WESTERN HATCHES (Hafele & Hughes; 1981, 223pp.), is a great book written specifically for the angler. It is a real gem, "An Angler's Entomology" guide which provides a detailed treatment of major western hacthes at the familiy and generic level in terms valuable to the angler. This book contains almost all the information an angler needs about the habitat and behavior of the major hatches, as well as patterns which match them. It also provides an introduction to entomology which is easily digested by the angler since it is presented with the fishermen in mind.

An Introduction To The AQUATIC INSECTS OF NORTH AMERICA, Second Edition (Merrit & Cummins editors; 1988, 722pp.), serves as a standard reference on the biology and ecology of aquatic insects with generic keys to seperate life stages of the major Orders. It also provides summaries of related information on morphology, methods, techniques, sampling and rearing, life history, behavior, respiration, and phylogeny of aquatic insects. It is written with the entomoligist rather then angler in mind, but it is indespensible to anglers interested in aquatic insects. It will allow you to accurrately identify almost any aquatic insect you collect to its genus, and its generic keys are very good and easy to use (As far as using keys goes) because comparative illustrations of morphological features are provided for each step of the key.

The remainder of this section provides a brief set of characteristics that are usefull in distinquishing the life stage and order of an aquatic insect in the field. If you are experienced these will be second nature, and if your learning you'll be able to recognize the orders at a glance once you've become familiar with these characteristics. More detailed information is available in the above mentioned books, as well as a number of pocket size angling entomology guides available on the market. Also provided, is a general Hatch Calendar for the west, which presents generalized emergence periods for some major hatches of the pacific north west.

PLECOPTERA (STONEFLIES)
Incomplete Metamorphosis

<u>Nymphs</u>
- Two stout tails
- Two claws on end of each leg
- Two antennae
- Gills may be absent or present as tufts or filaments on underside of head, thorax or abdomen.
- Generally good crawlers but poor swimmers

<u>Adults</u>
- Two stout tails, may be short with only one segment or long with many segements.
- Two claws on end of each leg
- Two long antennae
- Two pairs of equal size wings with many veins, held folded flat over back when at rest
- Relatively slow straight flight

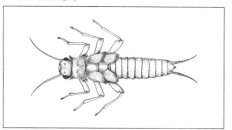

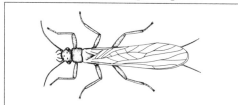

EPHEMEROPTERA (MAYFLIES)
Incomplete Metamorphosis

<u>Nymphs</u>
- Three cerci, some with middle tail reduced or absent
- One claw on end of each leg
- Two antennae
- Gills can be plate-like, filamentous, feathery, or tuning-forked shaped; but only present on abdomen.
- Behavior Variable depending on functional grouping: Swimmers-fast, active swimmers; Crawlers-crawl on bottom, slow swimmers; Clingers- cling to bottom, poor swimmers; Burrowers- burrow into bottom, moderate swimmers.

<u>Adults (subimago & imago)</u>
- Two or three long tails
- One claw on end of each leg
- Two short antennae
- Two pairs of wings with many veins, both pairs held vertically, front pair large and triangular, hind pair reduced or absent.
- Wings of subimago generally clowdy in appeearence while imago wings tend to be more clear
- Moderate straight flight.

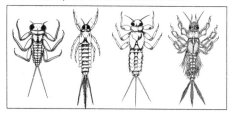

ODANATA (DRAGONFLIES & DAMSELFLIES)
Incomplete Metamorphosis

Nymphs
- Labium (lower lip) prehensile, able to extend outward to capture prey
- Two short antenae
- Large compound eyes
- Gills: dragonflies gills are internal rectal gills which are not visible; damsel flies have three leaf-like gills which resemble tails
- Body: Dragonflies are stout looking while damselflies are less robust
- Both are good crawlers, and moderate swimmers

Adults
- Two short antenae
- Large compound eyes
- Two pairs of large many veined wings, Dragonflies hold wings horizontally at right angle to body while at rest, damselfies hold wings together above body in a tent like fasion while at rest
- Long slender abdomen
- Fast excellant fliers, capable of helicopter like manuverability.

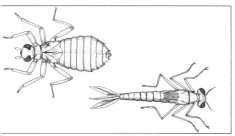

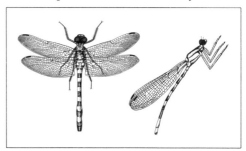

HEMIPTERA (BACKSWIMMERS & WATERBOATMEN)
Incomplete Metamorphosis

Nymphs & Adults similiar
- Two short antenae with four or five segments; greatly reduced or concealed in true aquatics
- Short slender beak mouth utilized in sucking fluids from prey
- Two pairs of wings with reduced venation; forwings thickened & leathery lying flat over abdomen covering membranous hindwings
- In true aquatics flight may not be possible or used only as escape from diminishing or degraded habitat; typically good swimmers, fast jerky motion, surfacing ocassionally for air

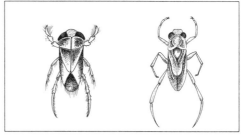

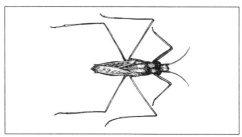

TRICHOPTERA (CADDISFLIES)
Complete Metamorphosis

<u>Larva</u>
- Two minute antenae, or absent
- Body slender with fleshy abdomen sclerotized (hardened) head and plates on thorax
- Anal legs/hooks present on last abdomenal segment, used for case attachment or backwards locomotion in non-casemaking forms
- Many forms build cases out of mineral or plant material, these may be a circular or rectangular tube, resemble a turtle or snail shell, or be absent in free living forms
- Attached or poor to moderate crawlers, moderate swimmers

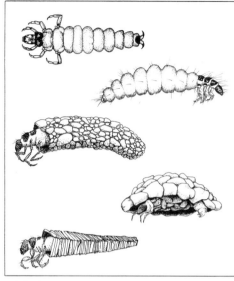

<u>Pupae</u>
- Two long antenae
- Wing pads present, well developed and slope under abdomen in late stages
- Hook bearing plates on top of abdomen in case-making forms
- Contained in silk cocoon inside of case or simply covering free living forms.
- Swim or crawl to surface depending on form

<u>Adults</u>
- Two long antenae, body length or greater.
- Two pairs of wings with simple venation: hindwings generally broader and shorter then forwings; held in tent-like fashion above admonen while at rest and covered with fine hairs
- Fast excellent fliers, fluttering

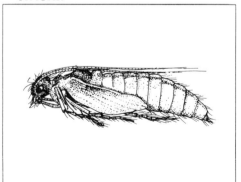

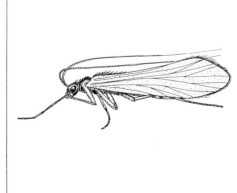

DIPTERA (TRUE FLIES)
Complete Metamorphosis

Larvae
- No true true jointed legs, although several prolegs (leg like appendages) may be present
- Head may be well developed, retracted, or absent entirely
- Body form generally resembles segmented tube
- Generally good crawlers or burrowers, poor swimmers

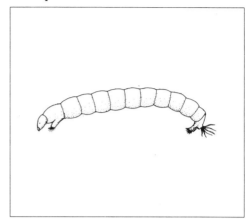

Pupae
- Head, thorax & wing case closely appressed or clumped together
- May be free living and active or contained in hard barrel shaped puparium
- Some good swimmers, propelled using abdomenal contractions towards head so that move in quick short jerks

Adults
- Two antanae, generally well formed but no longer then three times the width of the head
- Forwings well developed, hindwings reduced to slender club-shaped balancing organs
- Moderate to fast fliers

MEGALOPTERA (ALDERFLIES & DOBSINFLIES)
Complete Metamorphosis

Larvae
- Two short antanae
- Large well developed mandibles
- Last abdominal segment with either single long filament or a pair of hooks
- Pair of lateral filaments on each abdominal segment
- Poor swimmers

Pupae
- Pupation occurs on the shore itself or in decaying matter, pupa are not available to fish

Adults
- Two long antanae with bead-like segments
- Two pair of similar wings with heavy venation, held tent-like over abdomen, hairless
- Awkward to poor fliers

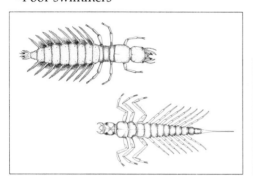

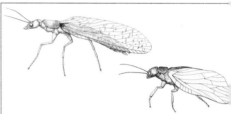

COLEOPTERA (WATER BEETLES)
Complete Metamorphosis

Larvae
- No tails, but may have caudal breathing tubes covered with stout tails which resemble tails
- One or two claws at end of each leg
- Forms without caudal breathing tubes may have gill filaments on abdomen
- Generally good crawlers, fair swim mers

Pupae
- Generally terrestrial and not avail able to fish

Adults
- Two antenae, long or short, some club-shaped at end
- Forwings are hard and lay over abdomencovering hindwings
- Moderate, somewhat lumbering fliers

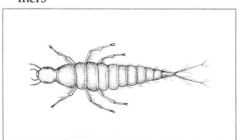

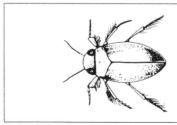

GENERAL HATCH CALENDAR FOR THE MOST COMMON HATCHES OF THE P.N.W.

IDENTIFICATION	PERIOD OF EMERGENCE.												TIME OF ACTIVITY
	J	F	M	A	M	J	J	A	S	O	N	D	
CHIRONOMIDAE	▓	▓	▓	▓	▓	▓	▓	▓	▓	▓			Through Out Day
Small Winter Stone	▓	▓											Mid Day
Blue Wing Olive		▓	▓	▓	▓	▓	▓	▓	▓				Late Morning to Late Afternoon
March Brown			▓	▓	▓	▓							Late Morning to Afternoon
Blue Dun			▓	▓	▓	▓	▓	▓	▓	▓			Late Morning to Afternoon
Little Yellow-May			▓	▓	▓	▓	▓						Mid Morning to Mid Day
Black Drake				▓	▓	▓							Mid Day
Giant Stone				▓	▓	▓							Through Out Day (Night Emergence)
Little Yellow Stone				▓	▓	▓	▓	▓					Late Morning Through Afternoon
Golden Stone				▓	▓	▓	▓						Through Out Day (Night Emergence)
Callibaetis				▓	▓	▓	▓	▓	▓				Mid Morning to Afternoon
Spotted Sedge					▓	▓	▓	▓	▓				Late Morning to Dusk
Ameletus					▓	▓	▓	▓					Mid Morning to Mid Afternoon
Pale Morning Dun					▓	▓	▓	▓					Mid Morning Through Afternoon
Drake (grandis)					▓	▓	▓						Mid Afternoon
Drake (doddsi)					▓	▓	▓	▓					Early Afternoon
Damsel Flies						▓	▓	▓					Late Morning Through Afternoon
Fall Caddis						▓	▓	▓	▓				Late Morning Through Dusk
Big Yellow-May							▓	▓					Late Evening Into The Night
Isonchia								▓	▓	▓			Late Afternoon to Evening
October Caddis									▓	▓			Late Morning Through Dusk
Terrestrials													
Ants				▓	▓	▓	▓	▓	▓				All Day (occurs after first 10 days above 70° in spring)
Grass Hopers						▓	▓	▓					Mid Afternoon Through Heat of the Day

SUGGESTED ABBREVIATIONS

ACTIVITY

H	Heavy
M	Moderate
LI	Light
S	Sporadic
N	None

HO	Holding
MO	Moving
FE	Feeding
RI	Rising
SP	Spawning
MF	Mating Flight

STAGE

E	Early
MI	Middle
L	Late
?	Unknown

NY	Nymph
LA	Larva
PU	Pupa
AD	Adult
SI	Subimago
IM	Imago
IN	Instar
CR	Crawler
CL	Clinger
SW	Swimmer
BU	Burrower

WATER

FA	Fast
ME	Medium
SL	Slow
ST	Still

P	Pool
R	Riffle
G	Glide
R	Rapid
PW	Pocket Water
F	Flat
BE	Back Eddy
UB	Undercut Bank

SU	Surface
MW	Midwater
B	Bottom
SH	Shallow
D	Deep
LE	Ledge/Shelf

FISH

OM	Rainbow Trout
OC	Cutthroat Trout
SF	Brook Trout
ST	Brown Trout
SC	Bull Trout
SN	Lake Trout
PW	White Fish
SS	Atlantic Salmon

OMA	Stealhead
OT	Chinook
OKI	Coho
ON	Sockeye
OKE	Chum
OCA	Blueback
AS	Shad

MS	Large Mouth
MD	Small Mouth
LS	Perch
PS	Crappie

MISC.

♂	Male
♀	Female
N/A	Not Applicable
N/M	Not Measured
EST	Estimated

ADDITIONS

_____ " _____
_____ " _____
_____ " _____
_____ " _____
_____ " _____
_____ " _____
_____ " _____
_____ " _____
_____ " _____
_____ " _____
_____ " _____
_____ " _____
_____ " _____
_____ " _____
_____ " _____
_____ " _____
_____ " _____
_____ " _____
_____ " _____

DAILY RECORD # ________

LOCATION

Date: ________________ Stream/Lake: ____________________

State______County______________Section/Access________________

____

WEATHER

AIR TEMP: 100° 90° 80° 70° 60° 50° 40° 30°

SKY

WIND: N W E S

PRECIPITATION

- ☐ None
- ☐ Snow
- ☐ Drizzle
- ☐ Fog
- ☐ Showers
- ☐ Heavy Rain
- ☐ Thunderstorm

BARO-METER: ____.____ rising / falling / steady

HUMIDITY: ________%

Weather Notes:

WATER

H_20 TEMP: 80° 70° 60° 50° 40° 30°

LEVEL: High / Low — rising / falling / steady

CLARITY: Clear — Dirty

SIZE

CHARACTER

Water Notes:

NOTES & SKETCHES

FISHING JOURNAL

DAILY RECORD

TIME LINE   HATCHES   FISH

TIME LINE
6am
6am
4am
2am
12am
10pm
8pm
6pm
4pm
2pm
12pm
10am
8am
6am

HATCHES

TIME	WATER TYPE	ACTIVITY & OBSERVATIONS	STAGE	IDENTIFICATION				

FISH

#	TIME	SIZE	WATER TYPE	OBSERVATIONS & METHODS	PATTERN	SPECIES		

LOCATION

Date: _____ Stream/Lake: _____

State_____County_____Section/Access_____

WEATHER

| A I R | 100° 90° 80° 70° |
| T E M P | 60° 50° 40° 30° |

S K Y

BARO-METER

Weather Notes:

WIND

N

W ✦ E

S

PRECIPITATION

☐ None ☐ Snow
☐ Drizzle ☐ Fog
☐ Showers
☐ Heavy Rain
☐ Thunderstorm

rising ↑ ↓ falling
↔ steady

HUMIDITY

_____ %

WATER

H₂0

| T E M P | 80° 70° 60° 50° 40° 30° |

L E V E L

High

Low

rising ↑ ↓ falling
↔ steady

CLARITY

Clear ▨▨▨▨▨ Dirty

SIZE | CHARACTER

Water Notes:

NOTES & SKETCHES

FISHING JOURNAL

TIME LINE

6am 8am 10am 12pm 2pm 4pm 6pm 8pm 10pm 12am 2am 4am 6am

6am 8am 10am 12pm 2pm 4pm 6pm 8pm 10pm 12am 2am 4am 6am

HATCHES

TIME					
WATER TYPE					
ACTIVITY & OBSERVATIONS					
STAGE					
IDENTIFICATION					

FISH

#					
TIME					
SIZE					
WATER TYPE					
OBSERVATIONS & METHODS					
PATTERN					
SPECIES					

18

ISHING JOURNAL   *DAILY RECORD #* _____

LOCATION

Date: _____   Stream/Lake: _____

State_____County_____Section/Access_____

WEATHER

A I R T E M P	100° 90° 80° 70° 60° 50° 40° 30°	S K Y		BARO-METER	Weather Notes:

AIR TEMP 100° 90° 80° 70° 60° 50° 40° 30°

SKY

BARO-METER

Weather Notes:

WIND
N
W — E
S

PRECIPITATION
☐ None   ☐ Snow
☐ Drizzle   ☐ Fog
☐ Showers
☐ Heavy Rain
☐ Thunderstorm

rising falling steady

HUMIDITY
_____ %

WATER

H_2O TEMP   80° 70° 60° 50° 40° 30°

L E V E L   High ... Low

rising falling steady

CLARITY
Clear   Dirty

Water Notes:

SIZE   CHARACTER

NOTES & SKETCHES

TIME LINE

HATCHES

FISH

TIME LINE: 6am 8am 10am 12pm 2pm 4pm 6pm 8pm 10pm 12am 2am 4am 6am

HATCHES columns: TIME | WATER TYPE | ACTIVITY & OBSERVATIONS | STAGE | IDENTIFICATION

FISH columns: # | TIME | SIZE | WATER TYPE | OBSERVATIONS & METHODS | PATTERN | SPECIES

LOCATION

Date: _____ Stream/Lake: _____

State_____County_____Section/Access_____

WEATHER

A I R

T E M P

100°
90°
80°
70°
60°
50°
40°
30°

S K Y

BARO-METER

rising falling steady

Weather Notes:

WIND

N
W   E
S

PRECIPITATION

☐ None   ☐ Snow
☐ Drizzle   ☐ Fog
☐ Showers
☐ Heavy Rain
☐ Thunderstorm

HUMIDITY

_____%

WATER

H₂0

T E M P

80°
70°
60°
50°
40°
30°

L E V E L

High

Low

rising falling steady

CLARITY

Clear   Dirty

SIZE   CHARACTER

Water Notes:

NOTES & SKETCHES

FISHING JOURNAL

DAILY RECORD

TIME LINE	HATCHES	FISH

TIME LINE

6am
4am
2am
12am
10pm
8pm
6pm
4pm
2pm
12pm
10am
8am
6am

HATCHES

TIME	WATER TYPE	ACTIVITY & OBSERVATIONS	STAGE	IDENTIFICATION

FISH

#	TIME	SIZE	WATER TYPE	OBSERVATIONS & METHODS	PATTERN	SPECIES

LOCATION

Date: _____   Stream/Lake: _____

State_____County_____Section/Access_____

WEATHER

A I R T E M P
100° 90° 80° 70° 60° 50° 40° 30°

S K Y

BARO-METER

____.____

rising   falling
steady

Weather Notes:

WIND
N
W — E
S

PRECIPITATION
☐ None   ☐ Snow
☐ Drizzle   ☐ Fog
☐ Showers
☐ Heavy Rain
☐ Thunderstorm

HUMIDITY
_____ %

WATER

H₂0

T E M P
80° 70° 60° 50° 40° 30°

L E V E L
High
Low
rising   falling
steady

CLARITY
Clear   Dirty

SIZE   CHARACTER

Water Notes:

NOTES & SKETCHES

FISHING JOURNAL

DAILY RECORD

TIME LINE

6am	8am	10am	12pm	2pm	4pm	6pm	8pm	10pm	12am	2am	4am	6am

HATCHES

TIME	WATER TYPE	ACTIVITY & OBSERVATIONS	STAGE	IDENTIFICATION

FISH

#	TIME	SIZE	WATER TYPE	OBSERVATIONS & METHODS	PATTERN	SPECIES

ISHING JOURNAL   *DAILY RECORD* # _____

LOCATION

Date: _____ Stream/Lake: _____
State_____County_____Section/Access_____
_____

WEATHER

A I R T E M P	100° 90° 80° 70° 60° 50° 40° 30°	S K Y			BARO-METER	Weather Notes:

AIR TEMP 100° 90° 80° 70° 60° 50° 40° 30°

S K Y

BARO-METER

Weather Notes:

WIND
N
W ◇ E
S

PRECIPITATION
☐ None   ☐ Snow
☐ Drizzle ☐ Fog
☐ Showers
☐ Heavy Rain
☐ Thunderstorm

rising ↑ ↓ falling
steady

HUMIDITY
_____%

WATER

H₂0 TEMP 80° 70° 60° 50° 40° 30°

L E V E L
High
Low
rising ↑ ↓ falling
steady

CLARITY
Clear   Dirty

SIZE   CHARACTER

Water Notes:

NOTES & SKETCHES

25

TIME LINE

HATCHES

FISH

TIME LINE

6am 4am 2am 12am 10pm 8pm 6pm 4pm 2pm 12pm 10am 8am 6am

HATCHES

TIME

WATER TYPE

ACTIVITY & OBSERVATIONS

STAGE

IDENTIFICATION

FISH

#

TIME

SIZE

WATER TYPE

OBSERVATIONS & METHODS

PATTERN

SPECIES

LOCATION

Date: _____   Stream/Lake: _____

State_____County_____Section/Access_____

WEATHER

A I R		S K Y				BARO-METER	Weather Notes:

AIR TEMP
100° 90° 80° 70° 60° 50° 40° 30°

WIND
N W E S

PRECIPITATION
- [ ] None
- [ ] Drizzle
- [ ] Showers
- [ ] Heavy Rain
- [ ] Thunderstorm
- [ ] Snow
- [ ] Fog

rising falling steady

BARO-METER ._____

HUMIDITY _____%

WATER

H₂0 TEMP
80° 70° 60° 50° 40° 30°

LEVEL High Low
rising falling steady

CLARITY
Clear ———— Dirty

SIZE | CHARACTER

Water Notes:

NOTES & SKETCHES

FISHING JOURNAL

DAILY RECORD

TIME LINE

HATCHES

FISH

6am 8am 10am 12pm 2pm 4pm 6pm 8pm 10pm 12am 2am 4am 6am

TIME

WATER TYPE

ACTIVITY & OBSERVATIONS

STAGE

IDENTIFICATION

\#

TIME

SIZE

WATER TYPE

OBSERVATIONS & METHODS

PATTERN

SPECIES

LOCATION

Date: _____ Stream/Lake: _____

State_____County_____Section/Access_____

WEATHER

A I R   T E M P

100°
90°
80°
70°
60°
50°
40°
30°

S K Y

BARO-METER

rising falling
steady

Weather Notes:

WIND

N

W ✧ E

S

PRECIPITATION

☐ None   ☐ Snow
☐ Drizzle   ☐ Fog
☐ Showers
☐ Heavy Rain   HUMIDITY
☐ Thunderstorm _____%

WATER

H₂0

T E M P

80°
70°
60°
50°
40°
30°

L E V E L

High

Low

rising falling
steady

CLARITY

Clear   Dirty

SIZE   CHARACTER

Water Notes:

NOTES & SKETCHES

FISHING JOURNAL

TIME LINE   HATCHES   FISH

TIME LINE

6am 8am 10am 12pm 2pm 4pm 6pm 8pm 10pm 12am 2am 4am 6am

HATCHES

TIME | WATER TYPE | ACTIVITY & OBSERVATIONS | STAGE | IDENTIFICATION

FISH

| TIME | SIZE | WATER TYPE | OBSERVATIONS & METHODS | PATTERN | SPECIES

LOCATION

Date: _____ Stream/Lake: _____
State_____County_____Section/Access_____

WEATHER

| A I R | 100° 90° 80° 70° | S K Y | | | | BARO-METER | Weather Notes: |

AIR TEMP — 100° 90° 80° 70° 60° 50° 40° 30°

SKY

BARO-METER ___.___

WIND
N
W ◆ E
S

PRECIPITATION
☐ None ☐ Snow
☐ Drizzle ☐ Fog
☐ Showers
☐ Heavy Rain
☐ Thunderstorm

rising ↑ falling ↓ ↔ steady

HUMIDITY _____%

WATER

H₂0 TEMP — 80° 70° 60° 50° 40° 30°

LEVEL High ↕ Low
rising falling steady

CLARITY
Clear ▭ Dirty

SIZE | CHARACTER

Water Notes:

NOTES & SKETCHES

FISHING JOURNAL

DAILY RECORD

TIME LINE

| HATCHES | FISH |

TIME LINE: 6am 8am 10am 12pm 2pm 4pm 6pm 8pm 10pm 12am 2am 4am 6am

HATCHES: TIME | WATER TYPE | ACTIVITY & OBSERVATIONS | STAGE | IDENTIFICATION

FISH: # | TIME | SIZE | WATER TYPE | OBSERVATIONS & METHODS | PATTERN | SPECIES

32

LOCATION

Date: _____　Stream/Lake: _____

State_____County_____Section/Access_____

WEATHER

A I R　T E M P

100°
90°
80°
70°
60°
50°
40°
30°

S K Y

BARO-METER

Weather Notes:

WIND

N
W　E
S

PRECIPITATION

☐ None　☐ Snow
☐ Drizzle　☐ Fog
☐ Showers
☐ Heavy Rain
☐ Thunderstorm

rising ↑　↓ falling
←→ steady

HUMIDITY

_____%

WATER

H$_2$0　T E M P

80°
70°
60°
50°
40°
30°

L E V E L

High

Low

rising ↑　↓ falling
←→ steady

CLARITY

Clear　　　　　　　Dirty

Water Notes:

SIZE　CHARACTER

NOTES & SKETCHES

TIME LINE

6am 8am 10am 12pm 2pm 4pm 6pm 8pm 10pm 12am 2am 4am 6am

HATCHES

IDENTIFICATION	STAGE	ACTIVITY & OBSERVATIONS	WATER TYPE	TIME

FISH

SPECIES	PATTERN	OBSERVATIONS & METHODS	WATER TYPE	SIZE	TIME	#

ISHING JOURNAL

DAILY RECORD # _____

LOCATION

Date: _____ Stream/Lake: _____

State_____County_____Section/Access_____

WEATHER

A I R T E M P	100° 90° 80° 70° 60° 50° 40° 30°

S K Y

WIND
N
W ✦ E
S

PRECIPITATION
- [ ] None
- [ ] Drizzle
- [ ] Showers
- [ ] Heavy Rain
- [ ] Thunderstorm
- [ ] Snow
- [ ] Fog

BARO-METER

rising ↑ falling ↓
steady ↔

HUMIDITY
_____%

Weather Notes:

WATER

| H₂0 T E M P | 80° 70° 60° 50° 40° 30° |

L E V E L
High
Low
rising ↑ falling ↓
steady ↔

CLARITY
Clear _____ Dirty

SIZE | CHARACTER

Water Notes:

NOTES & SKETCHES

TIME LINE

6am
4am
2am
12am
10pm
8pm
6pm
4pm
2pm
12pm
10am
8am
6am

HATCHES

TIME
WATER TYPE
ACTIVITY & OBSERVATIONS
STAGE
IDENTIFICATION

FISH

#
TIME
SIZE
WATER TYPE
OBSERVATIONS & METHODS
PATTERN
SPECIES

ISHING JOURNAL   *DAILY RECORD # _____*

LOCATION

Date: _____ Stream/Lake: _____

State_____County_____Section/Access_____

_____

WEATHER

| A I R   T E M P | 100° 90° 80° 70° 60° 50° 40° 30° | S K Y | WIND   N W   E   S | PRECIPITATION ☐None ☐Drizzle ☐Showers ☐Heavy Rain ☐Thunderstorm | ☐Snow ☐Fog | BARO-METER   rising↑ ↓falling steady | Weather Notes: |

HUMIDITY _____%

WATER

H₂0 T E M P — 80° 70° 60° 50° 40° 30°

L E V E L — High / Low — rising↑ ↓falling steady

CLARITY — Clear → Dirty

SIZE   CHARACTER

Water Notes:

NOTES & SKETCHES

_____

37

TIME LINE

6am 8am 10am 12pm 2pm 4pm 6pm 8pm 10pm 12am 2am 4am 6am

HATCHES

TIME	WATER TYPE	ACTIVITY & OBSERVATIONS	STAGE	IDENTIFICATION

FISH

#	TIME	SIZE	WATER TYPE	OBSERVATIONS & METHODS	PATTERN	SPECIES

LOCATION

Date: _____ Stream/Lake: _____

State_____County_____Section/Access_____

WEATHER

A I R	100° 90° 80° 70°	S K Y		BARO-METER

T E M P   60° 50° 40° 30°

WIND

N
W ◆ E
S

PRECIPITATION

- [ ] None
- [ ] Drizzle
- [ ] Showers
- [ ] Heavy Rain
- [ ] Thunderstorm
- [ ] Snow
- [ ] Fog

rising ↑ ↓ falling
steady

HUMIDITY

_____%

Weather Notes:

WATER

H_2O

T E M P   80° 70° 60° 50° 40° 30°

L E V E L   High   Low

rising ↑ ↓ falling
steady

CLARITY

Clear   Dirty

SIZE   CHARACTER

Water Notes:

NOTES & SKETCHES

FISHING JOURNAL

TIME LINE

| 6am | 8am | 10am | 12pm | 2pm | 4pm | 6pm | 8pm | 10pm | 12am | 2am | 4am | 6am |

HATCHES

TIME	WATER TYPE	ACTIVITY & OBSERVATIONS	STAGE	IDENTIFICATION

FISH

#	TIME	SIZE	WATER TYPE	OBSERVATIONS & METHODS	PATTERN	SPECIES

LOCATION

Date: _____ Stream/Lake: _____

State_____County_____Section/Access_____

_____

WEATHER

| A I R   T E M P | 100° 90° 80° 70° 60° 50° 40° 30° | S K Y | | BARO- METER | | Weather Notes: |

WIND
N
W — E
S

PRECIPITATION
☐ None   ☐ Snow
☐ Drizzle   ☐ Fog
☐ Showers
☐ Heavy Rain
☐ Thunderstorm

rising ↑   falling ↓
steady

HUMIDITY
_____%

WATER

H₂0

T E M P   80° 70° 60° 50° 40° 30°

L E V E L   High / Low

rising ↑   falling ↓
steady

CLARITY
Clear ———————————————— Dirty

SIZE   CHARACTER

Water Notes:

NOTES & SKETCHES

_____
_____
_____
_____
_____
_____
_____
_____
_____
_____
_____
_____
_____
_____

FISHING JOURNAL

DAILY RECORD

TIME LINE

HATCHES

FISH

6am 8am 10am 12pm 2pm 4pm 6pm 8pm 10pm 12am 2am 4am 6am

TIME

WATER TYPE

ACTIVITY & OBSERVATIONS

STAGE

IDENTIFICATION

#

TIME

SIZE

WATER TYPE

OBSERVATIONS & METHODS

PATTERN

SPECIES

42

LOCATION

Date: _____ Stream/Lake: _____

State_____County_____Section/Access_____

WEATHER

AIR TEMP

100°
90°
80°
70°
60°
50°
40°
30°

SKY

BARO-METER

WIND

N

W ◆ E

S

rising | falling | steady

PRECIPITATION

☐ None ☐ Snow
☐ Drizzle ☐ Fog
☐ Showers
☐ Heavy Rain
☐ Thunderstorm

HUMIDITY

_____%

Weather Notes:

WATER

H₂0 TEMP

80°
70°
60°
50°
40°
30°

LEVEL

High

Low

rising | falling | steady

CLARITY

Clear   Dirty

SIZE | **CHARACTER**

Water Notes:

NOTES & SKETCHES

FISHING JOURNAL

TIME LINE

6am
8am
10am
12pm
2pm
4pm
6pm
8pm
10pm
12am
2am
4am
6am

HATCHES

TIME						
WATER TYPE						
ACTIVITY & OBSERVATIONS						
STAGE						
IDENTIFICATION						

FISH

#					
TIME					
SIZE					
WATER TYPE					
OBSERVATIONS & METHODS					
PATTERN					
SPECIES					

44

LOCATION

Date: _____   Stream/Lake: _____

State_____County_____Section/Access_____

WEATHER

A I R T E M P	100° 90° 80° 70° 60° 50° 40° 30°	S K Y	BARO-METER	Weather Notes:

WIND
N
W ◆ E
S

PRECIPITATION
- [ ] None
- [ ] Drizzle
- [ ] Showers
- [ ] Heavy Rain
- [ ] Thunderstorm
- [ ] Snow
- [ ] Fog

rising / falling / steady

HUMIDITY

_____%

WATER

H₂0 — H_2O

T E M P	80° 70° 60° 50° 40° 30°	L E V E L	High Low	CLARITY	Water Notes:

rising / falling / steady

Clear   CLARITY   Dirty

SIZE	CHARACTER

NOTES & SKETCHES

FISHING JOURNAL

DAILY RECORD

TIME LINE

HATCHES

FISH

Time line markings	HATCHES columns	FISH columns
6am 8am 10am 12pm 2pm 4pm 6pm 8pm 10pm 12am 2am 4am 6am	TIME / WATER TYPE / ACTIVITY & OBSERVATIONS / STAGE / IDENTIFICATION	# / TIME / SIZE / WATER TYPE / OBSERVATIONS & METHODS / PATTERN / SPECIES

ISHING JOURNAL   *DAILY RECORD #* _____

LOCATION

Date: _____ Stream/Lake: _____
State_____ County_____ Section/Access_____

WEATHER

A I R		S K Y				BARO-METER	Weather Notes:

AIR TEMP 100° 90° 80° 70° 60° 50° 40° 30°

WIND N W E S

PRECIPITATION
- [ ] None
- [ ] Drizzle
- [ ] Showers
- [ ] Heavy Rain
- [ ] Thunderstorm
- [ ] Snow
- [ ] Fog

rising falling steady

HUMIDITY _____%

WATER

H₂0 TEMP 80° 70° 60° 50° 40° 30°

LEVEL High Low rising falling steady

CLARITY Clear Dirty

SIZE | CHARACTER

Water Notes:

NOTES & SKETCHES

47

FISHING JOURNAL

DAILY RECORD

TIME LINE

HATCHES

FISH

Time Line	
6am	
4am	
2am	
12am	
10pm	
8pm	
6pm	
4pm	
2pm	
12pm	
10am	
8am	
6am	

HATCHES table columns: TIME | WATER TYPE | ACTIVITY & OBSERVATIONS | STAGE | IDENTIFICATION

FISH table columns: # | TIME | SIZE | WATER TYPE | OBSERVATIONS & METHODS | PATTERN | SPECIES

ISHING JOURNAL   *DAILY RECORD #* _____

LOCATION

Date: _____ Stream/Lake: _____

State_____County_____Section/Access_____

WEATHER

A I R T E M P	100° 90° 80° 70° 60° 50° 40° 30°	S K Y			BARO-METER	Weather Notes:

WIND
N
W — E
S

PRECIPITATION
☐ None   ☐ Snow
☐ Drizzle   ☐ Fog
☐ Showers
☐ Heavy Rain
☐ Thunderstorm

rising falling steady

HUMIDITY _____%

WATER

H₂0   T E M P   80° 70° 60° 50° 40° 30°

L E V E L   High ... Low

rising falling steady

CLARITY
Clear ————————— Dirty

SIZE | CHARACTER

Water Notes:

NOTES & SKETCHES

FISHING JOURNAL

TIME LINE

6am 8am 10am 12pm 2pm 4pm 6pm 8pm 10pm 12am 2am 4am 6am

HATCHES

TIME	WATER TYPE	ACTIVITY & OBSERVATIONS	STAGE	IDENTIFICATION

FISH

#	TIME	SIZE	WATER TYPE	OBSERVATIONS & METHODS	PATTERN	SPECIES

50

LOCATION

Date: _____ Stream/Lake: _____

State_____County_____Section/Access_____

WEATHER

A I R		S K Y				BARO- METER	Weather Notes:

AIR TEMP: 100° 90° 80° 70° 60° 50° 40° 30°

WIND

N
W — E
S

PRECIPITATION

- [ ] None
- [ ] Drizzle
- [ ] Showers
- [ ] Heavy Rain
- [ ] Thunderstorm
- [ ] Snow
- [ ] Fog

rising / falling / steady

HUMIDITY _____%

WATER

H₂0 — H_2O

WATER TEMP: 80° 70° 60° 50° 40° 30°

LEVEL: High — Low

rising / falling / steady

CLARITY — Clear .... Dirty

SIZE | CHARACTER

Water Notes:

NOTES & SKETCHES

FISHING JOURNAL

TIME LINE   HATCHES   FISH

TIME LINE

6am 8am 10am 12pm 2pm 4pm 6pm 8pm 10pm 12am 2am 4am 6am

HATCHES

TIME	WATER TYPE	ACTIVITY & OBSERVATIONS	STAGE	IDENTIFICATION

FISH

#	TIME	SIZE	WATER TYPE	OBSERVATIONS & METHODS	PATTERN	SPECIES

ISHING JOURNAL   *DAILY RECORD #* _____

LOCATION

Date: _____ Stream/Lake: _____
State_____County_____Section/Access_____
_____

WEATHER

A I R   T E M P
100°
90°
80°
70°
60°
50°
40°
30°

S K Y

BARO-
METER

Weather Notes:

WIND
N
W ◆ E
S

PRECIPITATION
☐ None   ☐ Snow
☐ Drizzle   ☐ Fog
☐ Showers
☐ Heavy Rain
☐ Thunderstorm

rising falling steady

HUMIDITY
_____%

WATER

H₂0   T E M P
80°
70°
60°
50°
40°
30°

L E V E L
High
Low
rising falling steady

CLARITY
Clear   Dirty

Water Notes:

SIZE | CHARACTER

NOTES & SKETCHES

FISHING JOURNAL

TIME LINE

HATCHES

FISH

TIME	WATER TYPE	ACTIVITY & OBSERVATIONS	STAGE	IDENTIFICATION

Time line scale: 6am 8am 10am 12pm 2pm 4pm 6pm 8pm 10pm 12am 2am 4am 6am

#	TIME	SIZE	WATER TYPE	OBSERVATIONS & METHODS	PATTERN	SPECIES

LOCATION

Date: _____ Stream/Lake: _____

State_____County_____Section/Access_____

WEATHER

A I R	100° 90° 80° 70°

S K Y

BARO-METER

Weather Notes:

WIND

N

W   E

S

PRECIPITATION

- [ ] None
- [ ] Drizzle
- [ ] Showers
- [ ] Heavy Rain
- [ ] Thunderstorm

- [ ] Snow
- [ ] Fog

rising   falling   steady

HUMIDITY

_____%

T E M P   60° 50° 40° 30°

WATER

H_2O

T E M P   80° 70° 60° 50° 40° 30°

L E V E L   High   Low

rising falling steady

CLARITY

Clear   Dirty

SIZE   CHARACTER

Water Notes:

NOTES & SKETCHES

TIME LINE   HATCHES   FISH

TIME LINE
6am 8am 10am 12pm 2pm 4pm 6pm 8pm 10pm 12am 2am 4am 6am

HATCHES

TIME	WATER TYPE	ACTIVITY & OBSERVATIONS	STAGE	IDENTIFICATION

FISH

#	TIME	SIZE	WATER TYPE	OBSERVATIONS & METHODS	PATTERN	SPECIES

LOCATION

Date: _____ Stream/Lake: _____

State_____County_____Section/Access_____

WEATHER

A I R   T E M P

100°
90°
80°
70°
60°
50°
40°
30°

S K Y

BARO-METER

_____.___

rising falling
steady

Weather Notes:

WIND

N
W — E
S

PRECIPITATION

☐ None
☐ Drizzle
☐ Showers
☐ Heavy Rain
☐ Thunderstorm
☐ Snow
☐ Fog

HUMIDITY

_____ %

WATER

H₂0   T E M P

80°
70°
60°
50°
40°
30°

rising falling
steady

L E V E L

High

Low

CLARITY

Clear   Dirty

SIZE   CHARACTER

Water Notes:

NOTES & SKETCHES

TIME LINE   **HATCHES**   **FISH**

TIME LINE ruler: 6am 8am 10am 12pm 2pm 4pm 6pm 8pm 10pm 12am 2am 4am 6am

HATCHES columns:
- TIME
- WATER TYPE
- ACTIVITY & OBSERVATIONS
- STAGE
- IDENTIFICATION

FISH columns:
- #
- TIME
- SIZE
- WATER TYPE
- OBSERVATIONS & METHODS
- PATTERN
- SPECIES

LOCATION

Date: _____ Stream/Lake: _____

State_____County_____Section/Access_____

WEATHER

A I R   T E M P

100°
90°
80°
70°
60°
50°
40°
30°

S K Y

WIND

N

W — E

S

PRECIPITATION

☐ None   ☐ Snow
☐ Drizzle   ☐ Fog
☐ Showers
☐ Heavy Rain
☐ Thunderstorm

BARO-METER

rising ↑   ↓ falling

steady →←

HUMIDITY

_____%

Weather Notes:

WATER

H₂0

T E M P

80°
70°
60°
50°
40°
30°

L E V E L

High

Low

rising ↑   ↓ falling

steady →←

CLARITY

Clear   Dirty

SIZE   **CHARACTER**

Water Notes:

NOTES & SKETCHES

FISHING JOURNAL

DAILY RECORD

TIME LINE

6am 8am 10am 12pm 2pm 4pm 6pm 8pm 10pm 12am 2am 4am 6am

HATCHES

TIME
WATER TYPE
ACTIVITY & OBSERVATIONS
STAGE
IDENTIFICATION

FISH

#
TIME
SIZE
WATER TYPE
OBSERVATIONS & METHODS
PATTERN
SPECIES

LOCATION

Date: _____ Stream/Lake: _____

State_____County_____Section/Access_____

WEATHER

| A I R   T E M P | S K Y | WIND | PRECIPITATION | BARO-METER | Weather Notes: |

AIR TEMP
- 100°
- 90°
- 80°
- 70°
- 60°
- 50°
- 40°
- 30°

SKY

WIND
- N
- W
- E
- S

PRECIPITATION
- ☐ None
- ☐ Drizzle
- ☐ Showers
- ☐ Heavy Rain
- ☐ Thunderstorm
- ☐ Snow
- ☐ Fog

BARO-METER
._____

rising / steady / falling

HUMIDITY
_____ %

Weather Notes:

WATER

H_2O TEMP
- 80°
- 70°
- 60°
- 50°
- 40°
- 30°

LEVEL
- High
- Low

rising / steady / falling

CLARITY
Clear — Dirty

SIZE | CHARACTER

Water Notes:

NOTES & SKETCHES

FISHING JOURNAL

DAILY RECORD

TIME LINE   HATCHES   FISH

TIME LINE

6am 8am 10am 12pm 2pm 4pm 6pm 8pm 10pm 12am 2am 4am 6am

HATCHES

TIME	WATER TYPE	ACTIVITY & OBSERVATIONS	STAGE	IDENTIFICATION

FISH

#	TIME	SIZE	WATER TYPE	OBSERVATIONS & METHODS	PATTERN	SPECIES

62

LOCATION

Date: _____ Stream/Lake: _____

State_____County_____Section/Access_____

WEATHER

A I R — 100° 90° 80° 70°

T E M P — 60° 50° 40° 30°

SKY

WIND
N
W — E
S

PRECIPITATION
☐ None ☐ Snow
☐ Drizzle ☐ Fog
☐ Showers
☐ Heavy Rain
☐ Thunderstorm

BARO-METER
___.___
rising steady falling

HUMIDITY _____%

Weather Notes:

WATER

H₂0

T E M P — 80° 70° 60° 50° 40° 30°

LEVEL High / Low
rising steady falling

CLARITY
Clear ———— Dirty

SIZE | CHARACTER

Water Notes:

NOTES & SKETCHES

TIME LINE | HATCHES | FISH

TIME LINE

6am 8am 10am 12pm 2pm 4pm 6pm 8pm 10pm 12am 2am 4am 6am

HATCHES

TIME	WATER TYPE	ACTIVITY & OBSERVATIONS	STAGE	IDENTIFICATION

FISH

#	TIME	SIZE	WATER TYPE	OBSERVATIONS & METHODS	PATTERN	SPECIES

ISHING JOURNAL   *DAILY RECORD #* _____

Date: _____ Stream/Lake: _____

State_____County_____Section/Access_____

A I R   T E M P

100°
90°
80°
70°
60°
50°
40°
30°

S K Y

BARO-METER

__.__

rising falling steady

Weather Notes:

WIND

N
W — E
S

PRECIPITATION

☐ None   ☐ Snow
☐ Drizzle   ☐ Fog
☐ Showers
☐ Heavy Rain
☐ Thunderstorm

HUMIDITY

_____%

H₂0 T E M P

80°
70°
60°
50°
40°
30°

rising falling steady

L E V E L

High

Low

CLARITY

Clear   Dirty

Water Notes:

SIZE   CHARACTER

NOTES & SKETCHES

TIME LINE   HATCHES   FISH

TIME LINE (times listed): 6am, 4am, 2am, 12am, 10pm, 8pm, 6pm, 4pm, 2pm, 12pm, 10am, 8am, 6am, 6am

HATCHES columns: TIME, WATER TYPE, ACTIVITY & OBSERVATIONS, STAGE, IDENTIFICATION

FISH columns: #, TIME, SIZE, WATER TYPE, OBSERVATIONS & METHODS, PATTERN, SPECIES

LOCATION

Date: _____ Stream/Lake: _____

State_____County_____Section/Access_____

WEATHER

A I R　T E M P

100°
90°
80°
70°
60°
50°
40°
30°

S K Y

WIND

N
W　　E
S

PRECIPITATION

☐ None　　☐ Snow
☐ Drizzle　☐ Fog
☐ Showers
☐ Heavy Rain
☐ Thunderstorm

BARO-METER

rising ↑　↓ falling
↔ steady

HUMIDITY

_____%

Weather Notes:

WATER

H_2O　T E M P

80°
70°
60°
50°
40°
30°

L E V E L

High

Low

rising ↑　↓ falling
↔ steady

CLARITY

Clear　　　　　　　　Dirty

SIZE　　CHARACTER

Water Notes:

NOTES & SKETCHES

FISHING JOURNAL

DAILY RECORD

TIME LINE

6am	
4am	
2am	
12am	
10pm	
8pm	
6pm	
4pm	
2pm	
12pm	
10am	
8am	
6am	

HATCHES

TIME					
WATER TYPE					
ACTIVITY & OBSERVATIONS					
STAGE					
IDENTIFICATION					

FISH

#				
TIME				
SIZE				
WATER TYPE				
OBSERVATIONS & METHODS				
PATTERN				
SPECIES				

DAILY RECORD # _____

LOCATION

Date: _____ Stream/Lake: _____

State_____County_____Section/Access_____

WEATHER

A I R T E M P	100° 90° 80° 70° 60° 50° 40° 30°

S K Y

BARO-METER

Weather Notes:

WIND
N
W ◆ E
S

PRECIPITATION
☐ None ☐ Snow
☐ Drizzle ☐ Fog
☐ Showers
☐ Heavy Rain
☐ Thunderstorm

rising ↑ ↓ falling
← steady →

HUMIDITY
_____%

WATER

H₂0

T E M P 80° 70° 60° 50° 40° 30°

L E V E L High ─ Low

rising ↑ ↓ falling
steady

CLARITY
Clear ▬▬▬▬▬▬ Dirty

Water Notes:

SIZE | CHARACTER

NOTES & SKETCHES

TIME LINE

6am — 6am
4am
2am
12am
10pm
8pm
6pm
4pm
2pm
12pm
10am
8am
6am

HATCHES

TIME

WATER TYPE

ACTIVITY & OBSERVATIONS

STAGE

IDENTIFICATION

FISH

#

TIME

SIZE

WATER TYPE

OBSERVATIONS & METHODS

PATTERN

SPECIES

LOCATION

Date: _____ Stream/Lake: _____

State_____County_____Section/Access_____

WEATHER

A I R — T E M P

100°
90°
80°
70°
60°
50°
40°
30°

S K Y

BARO-METER

·___

Weather Notes:

WIND

N
W — E
S

PRECIPITATION

☐ None   ☐ Snow
☐ Drizzle   ☐ Fog
☐ Showers
☐ Heavy Rain
☐ Thunderstorm

rising ↑   ↓ falling
steady ↔

HUMIDITY

_____%

WATER

H₂0 — T E M P

80°
70°
60°
50°
40°
30°

L E V E L

High

Low

rising ↑ ↓ falling
steady ↔

Water Notes:

CLARITY

Clear   Dirty

SIZE   CHARACTER

NOTES & SKETCHES

TIME LINE

6am 8am 10am 12pm 2pm 4pm 6pm 8pm 10pm 12am 2am 4am 6am

HATCHES

TIME

WATER TYPE

ACTIVITY & OBSERVATIONS

STAGE

IDENTIFICATION

FISH

#

TIME

SIZE

WATER TYPE

OBSERVATIONS & METHODS

PATTERN

SPECIES

SHING JOURNAL   *DAILY RECORD* # _____

LOCATION

Date: _____ Stream/Lake: _____

State_____County_____Section/Access_____

_____

WEATHER

AIR TEMP
- 100°
- 90°
- 80°
- 70°
- 60°
- 50°
- 40°
- 30°

SKY

BAROMETER

Weather Notes:

WIND
N
W — E
S

PRECIPITATION
- [ ] None
- [ ] Drizzle
- [ ] Showers
- [ ] Heavy Rain
- [ ] Thunderstorm
- [ ] Snow
- [ ] Fog

rising / falling / steady

HUMIDITY _____%

WATER

H₂0 TEMP
- 80°
- 70°
- 60°
- 50°
- 40°
- 30°

LEVEL
High
Low

rising / falling / steady

CLARITY
Clear — Dirty

SIZE | CHARACTER

Water Notes:

NOTES & SKETCHES

73

TIME LINE

HATCHES

FISH

TIME LINE
6am
4am
2am
12am
10pm
8pm
6pm
4pm
2pm
12pm
10am
8am
6am

HATCHES

TIME	WATER TYPE	ACTIVITY & OBSERVATIONS	STAGE	IDENTIFICATION

FISH

#	TIME	SIZE	WATER TYPE	OBSERVATIONS & METHODS	PATTERN	SPECIES

LOCATION

Date: _____ Stream/Lake: _____

State_____County_____Section/Access_____

WEATHER

A I R   T E M P
100° 90° 80° 70° 60° 50° 40° 30°

S K Y

WIND
N
W — E
S

PRECIPITATION
☐ None ☐ Snow
☐ Drizzle ☐ Fog
☐ Showers
☐ Heavy Rain
☐ Thunderstorm

BARO-METER
_.___
rising steady falling

HUMIDITY
_____ %

Weather Notes:

WATER

H₂0   T E M P
80° 70° 60° 50° 40° 30°

L E V E L
High
Low
rising steady falling

CLARITY
Clear   Dirty

SIZE   CHARACTER

Water Notes:

NOTES & SKETCHES

FISHING JOURNAL

TIME LINE   HATCHES   FISH

TIME LINE

6am 8am 10am 12pm 2pm 4pm 6pm 8pm 10pm 12am 2am 4am 6am

HATCHES

TIME	WATER TYPE	ACTIVITY & OBSERVATIONS	STAGE	IDENTIFICATION

FISH

#	TIME	SIZE	WATER TYPE	OBSERVATIONS & METHODS	PATTERN	SPECIES

LOCATION

Date: _____ Stream/Lake: _____

State_____County_____Section/Access_____

WEATHER

A I R T E M P	100° 90° 80° 70° 60° 50° 40° 30°

S K Y

WIND
N
W — E
S

BARO-METER
._____

rising / falling / steady

PRECIPITATION
- [ ] None
- [ ] Drizzle
- [ ] Showers
- [ ] Heavy Rain
- [ ] Thunderstorm
- [ ] Snow
- [ ] Fog

HUMIDITY
_____%

Weather Notes:

WATER

H₂0 T E M P	80° 70° 60° 50° 40° 30°

L E V E L — High / Low

rising / falling / steady

CLARITY
Clear ———— Dirty

SIZE   CHARACTER

Water Notes:

NOTES & SKETCHES

FISHING JOURNAL

DAILY RECORD

TIME LINE   HATCHES   FISH

TIME LINE

6am · 8am · 10am · 12pm · 2pm · 4pm · 6pm · 8pm · 10pm · 12am · 2am · 4am · 6am

HATCHES

TIME						
WATER TYPE						
ACTIVITY & OBSERVATIONS						
STAGE						
IDENTIFICATION						

FISH

#					
TIME					
SIZE					
WATER TYPE					
OBSERVATIONS & METHODS					
PATTERN					
SPECIES					

78

LOCATION

Date: _____ Stream/Lake: _____

State_____County_____Section/Access_____

WEATHER

A I R	100° 90° 80° 70°	S K Y

SKY

BARO-METER

Weather Notes:

.____

T E M P	60° 50° 40° 30°	WIND	PRECIPITATION

N

W ◇ E

S

PRECIPITATION
- [ ] None
- [ ] Drizzle
- [ ] Showers
- [ ] Heavy Rain
- [ ] Thunderstorm
- [ ] Snow
- [ ] Fog

rising / falling / steady

HUMIDITY

_____%

WATER

H₂0

T E M P	80° 70° 60° 50° 40° 30°	L E V E L	High / Low

rising / falling / steady

CLARITY

Clear ▬▬▬▬▬▬▬▬ Dirty

Water Notes:

SIZE | CHARACTER

NOTES & SKETCHES

_____

_____

_____

_____

_____

_____

_____

_____

_____

_____

_____

_____

_____

_____

FISHING JOURNAL

DAILY RECORD

TIME LINE

HATCHES

FISH

6am 8am 10am 12pm 2pm 4pm 6pm 8pm 10pm 12am 2am 4am 6am

TIME
WATER TYPE
ACTIVITY & OBSERVATIONS
STAGE
IDENTIFICATION

#
TIME
SIZE
WATER TYPE
OBSERVATIONS & METHODS
PATTERN
SPECIES

LOCATION

Date: _____ Stream/Lake: _____
State_____County_____Section/Access_____
_____

WEATHER

A I R T E M P
100° 90° 80° 70° 60° 50° 40° 30°

S K Y

BARO-METER

Weather Notes:

WIND
N
W — E
S

PRECIPITATION
- [ ] None
- [ ] Drizzle
- [ ] Showers
- [ ] Heavy Rain
- [ ] Thunderstorm
- [ ] Snow
- [ ] Fog

rising / falling / steady

HUMIDITY
_____%

WATER

H_2O T E M P
80° 70° 60° 50° 40° 30°

L E V E L
High / Low
rising / falling / steady

CLARITY
Clear — Dirty

SIZE | CHARACTER

Water Notes:

NOTES & SKETCHES

TIME LINE   HATCHES   FISH

TIME LINE

6am 8am 10am 12pm 2pm 4pm 6pm 8pm 10pm 12am 2am 4am 6am

HATCHES

TIME	WATER TYPE	ACTIVITY & OBSERVATIONS	STAGE	IDENTIFICATION

FISH

#	TIME	SIZE	WATER TYPE	OBSERVATIONS & METHODS	PATTERN	SPECIES

LOCATION

Date: _____ Stream/Lake: _____

State_____County_____Section/Access_____

WEATHER

AIR TEMP

100°
90°
80°
70°
60°
50°
40°
30°

SKY

BARO-METER

rising / falling / steady

Weather Notes:

WIND

N
W ⟡ E
S

PRECIPITATION

☐ None   ☐ Snow
☐ Drizzle   ☐ Fog
☐ Showers
☐ Heavy Rain
☐ Thunderstorm

HUMIDITY

_____ %

WATER

H_2O **TEMP**

80°
70°
60°
50°
40°
30°

LEVEL

High

Low

rising / falling / steady

CLARITY

Clear ▬▬▬▬▬▬▬▬ Dirty

SIZE | **CHARACTER**

Water Notes:

NOTES & SKETCHES

FISHING JOURNAL

DAILY RECORD

TIME LINE   HATCHES   FISH

TIME	WATER TYPE	ACTIVITY & OBSERVATIONS	STAGE	IDENTIFICATION

Time line: 6am 8am 10am 12pm 2pm 4pm 6pm 8pm 10pm 12am 2am 4am 6am

#	TIME	SIZE	WATER TYPE	OBSERVATIONS & METHODS	PATTERN	SPECIES

ISHING JOURNAL   *DAILY RECORD* # _____

LOCATION

Date: _____ Stream/Lake: _____

State_____County_____Section/Access_____

WEATHER

A I R   T E M P
100° 90° 80° 70° 60° 50° 40° 30°

S K Y

WIND
N
W—E
S

PRECIPITATION
- [ ] None
- [ ] Drizzle
- [ ] Showers
- [ ] Heavy Rain
- [ ] Thunderstorm
- [ ] Snow
- [ ] Fog

BARO-METER
rising / falling / steady

HUMIDITY
_____%

Weather Notes:

WATER

H₂0
T E M P
80° 70° 60° 50° 40° 30°

LEVEL
High
Low
rising / falling / steady

CLARITY
Clear ———— Dirty

SIZE   CHARACTER

Water Notes:

NOTES & SKETCHES

85

TIME LINE | HATCHES | FISH

TIME LINE

6am 8am 10am 12pm 2pm 4pm 6pm 8pm 10pm 12am 2am 4am 6am

HATCHES

TIME	WATER TYPE	ACTIVITY & OBSERVATIONS	STAGE	IDENTIFICATION

FISH

#	TIME	SIZE	WATER TYPE	OBSERVATIONS & METHODS	PATTERN	SPECIES

LOCATION

Date: _____ Stream/Lake: _____

State_____County_____Section/Access_____

WEATHER

A I R	100° 90° 80° 70°	S K Y				BARO-METER	Weather Notes:

A I R T E M P — 100° 90° 80° 70° 60° 50° 40° 30°

S K Y

BARO-METER

rising falling

steady

WIND

N

W   E

S

PRECIPITATION

☐ None   ☐ Snow
☐ Drizzle ☐ Fog
☐ Showers
☐ Heavy Rain
☐ Thunderstorm

HUMIDITY

_____%

Weather Notes:

WATER

H₂0

T E M P — 80° 70° 60° 50° 40° 30°

L E V E L

High

Low

rising falling

steady

CLARITY

Clear   Dirty

SIZE   CHARACTER

Water Notes:

NOTES & SKETCHES

TIME LINE

HATCHES

FISH

TIME LINE scale (vertical): 6am, 8am, 10am, 12pm, 2pm, 4pm, 6pm, 8pm, 10pm, 12am, 2am, 4am, 6am

HATCHES columns: TIME | WATER TYPE | ACTIVITY & OBSERVATIONS | STAGE | IDENTIFICATION

FISH columns: # | TIME | SIZE | WATER TYPE | OBSERVATIONS & METHODS | PATTERN | SPECIES

ISHING JOURNAL   *DAILY RECORD* # _____

LOCATION

Date: _____ Stream/Lake: _____
State_____County_____Section/Access_____

WEATHER

A I R   T E M P

100° 90° 80° 70° 60° 50° 40° 30°

S K Y

WIND
N
W — E
S

BARO-METER

Weather Notes:

PRECIPITATION
☐ None   ☐ Snow
☐ Drizzle   ☐ Fog
☐ Showers
☐ Heavy Rain
☐ Thunderstorm

rising ↑ ↓ falling ↔ steady

HUMIDITY
_____%

WATER

H₂0 T E M P

80° 70° 60° 50° 40° 30°

L E V E L

High
Low

rising ↑ ↓ falling ↔ steady

CLARITY
Clear   Dirty

SIZE   CHARACTER

Water Notes:

NOTES & SKETCHES

TIME LINE

HATCHES

FISH

TIME LINE: 6am 8am 10am 12pm 2pm 4pm 6pm 8pm 10pm 12am 2am 4am 6am

HATCHES columns: TIME | WATER TYPE | ACTIVITY & OBSERVATIONS | STAGE | IDENTIFICATION

FISH columns: # | TIME | SIZE | WATER TYPE | OBSERVATIONS & METHODS | PATTERN | SPECIES

LOCATION

Date: _____ Stream/Lake: _____
State_____County_____Section/Access_____
_____

WEATHER

A I R T E M P	100° 90° 80° 70° 60° 50° 40° 30°

S K Y

BARO-METER

_____ . _____

rising ↑   ↓ falling
steady →

Weather Notes:

WIND

N
W ✦ E
S

PRECIPITATION

☐ None   ☐ Snow
☐ Drizzle   ☐ Fog
☐ Showers
☐ Heavy Rain
☐ Thunderstorm

HUMIDITY

_____ %

WATER

H$_2$0   T E M P | 80° 70° 60° 50° 40° 30° |

L E V E L

High
Low

rising ↑   ↓ falling
steady →

CLARITY

Clear   Dirty

Water Notes:

SIZE	CHARACTER

NOTES & SKETCHES

_____
_____
_____
_____
_____
_____
_____
_____
_____
_____
_____
_____
_____
_____

TIME LINE   HATCHES   FISH

TIME LINE

6am 8am 10am 12pm 2pm 4pm 6pm 8pm 10pm 12am 2am 4am 6am

HATCHES

TIME

WATER TYPE

ACTIVITY & OBSERVATIONS

STAGE

IDENTIFICATION

FISH

#

TIME

SIZE

WATER TYPE

OBSERVATIONS & METHODS

PATTERN

SPECIES

ISHING JOURNAL   *DAILY RECORD* # _____

LOCATION

Date: _____ Stream/Lake: _____
State_____County_____Section/Access_____

WEATHER

A I R   T E M P
100° 90° 80° 70° 60° 50° 40° 30°

S K Y

BARO-METER
_____._____

Weather Notes:

WIND
N
W — E
S

PRECIPITATION
☐ None   ☐ Snow
☐ Drizzle   ☐ Fog
☐ Showers
☐ Heavy Rain
☐ Thunderstorm

rising / falling / steady

HUMIDITY
_____%

WATER

H₂0   T E M P
80° 70° 60° 50° 40° 30°

L E V E L
High
Low
rising / falling / steady

CLARITY
Clear   Dirty

SIZE | CHARACTER

Water Notes:

NOTES & SKETCHES

FISHING JOURNAL

TIME LINE

HATCHES

FISH

TIME LINE

6am 8am 10am 12pm 2pm 4pm 6pm 8pm 10pm 12am 2am 4am 6am

HATCHES

TIME							
WATER TYPE							
ACTIVITY & OBSERVATIONS							
STAGE							
IDENTIFICATION							

FISH

#					
TIME					
SIZE					
WATER TYPE					
OBSERVATIONS & METHODS					
PATTERN					
SPECIES					

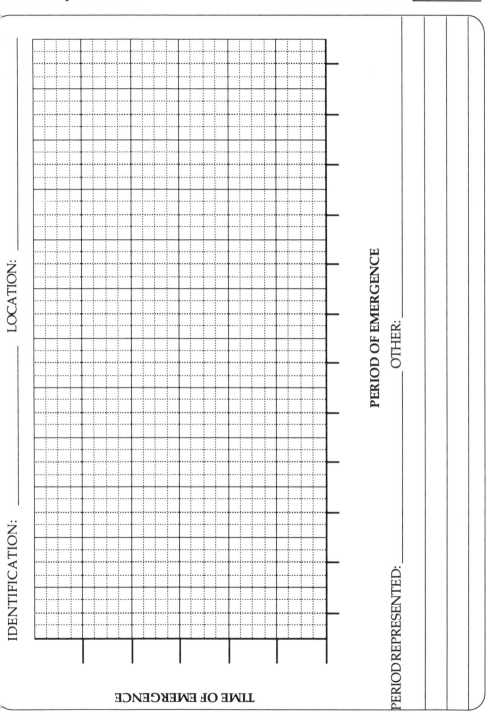

LOCATION: _____

IDENTIFICATION: _____

PERIOD OF EMERGENCE

OTHER: _____

PERIOD REPRESENTED: _____

TIME OF EMERGENCE

RECORD	DATE	TIME RANGE	TEMP RANGE		OTHER
			WATER	AIR	

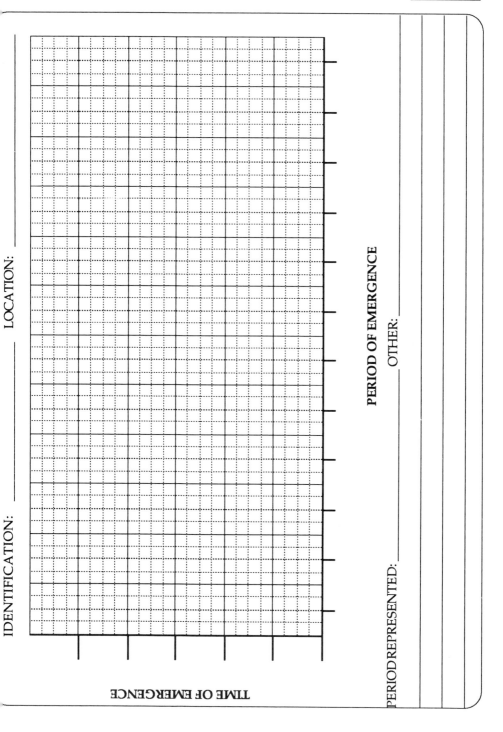

LOCATION: _____

IDENTIFICATION: _____

PERIOD OF EMERGENCE   OTHER: _____

PERIOD REPRESENTED: _____

TIME OF EMERGENCE

FISHING JOURNAL

RECORD	DATE	TIME RANGE	TEMP RANGE		OTHER
			WATER	AIR	

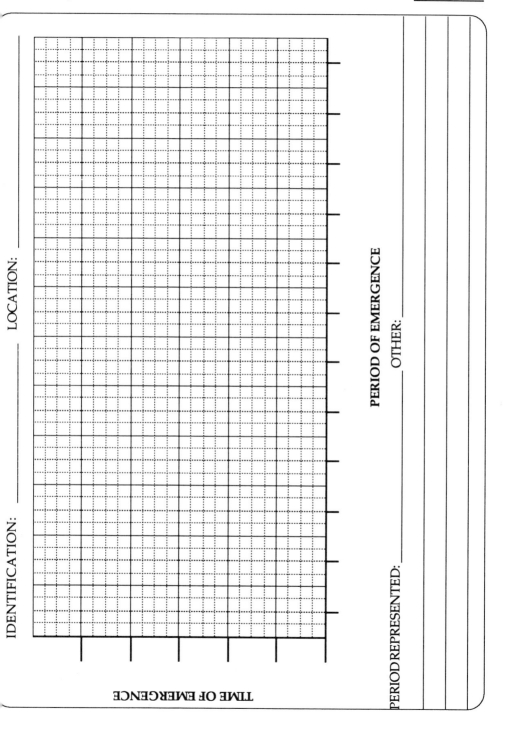

LOCATION: _____

IDENTIFICATION: _____

TIME OF EMERGENCE

PERIOD OF EMERGENCE

OTHER: _____

PERIOD REPRESENTED: _____

RECORD	DATE	TIME RANGE	TEMP RANGE		OTHER
			WATER	AIR	

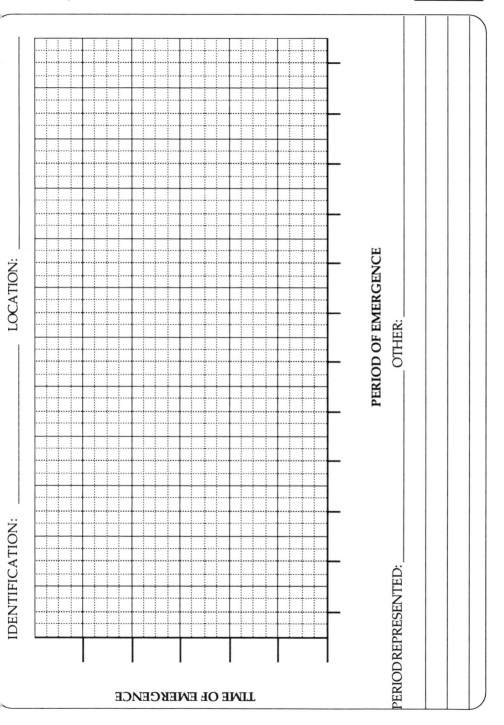

LOCATION: _____

IDENTIFICATION: _____

PERIOD OF EMERGENCE

OTHER: _____

PERIOD REPRESENTED: _____

TIME OF EMERGENCE

RECORD	DATE	TIME RANGE	TEMP RANGE		OTHER
			WATER	AIR	

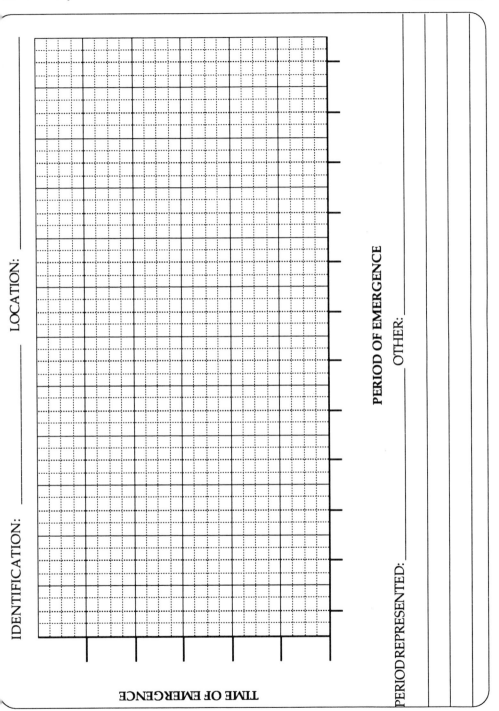

LOCATION: _____

IDENTIFICATION: _____

TIME OF EMERGENCE

PERIOD OF EMERGENCE

OTHER: _____

PERIOD REPRESENTED: _____

RECORD	DATE	TIME RANGE	TEMP RANGE		OTHER
			WATER	AIR	

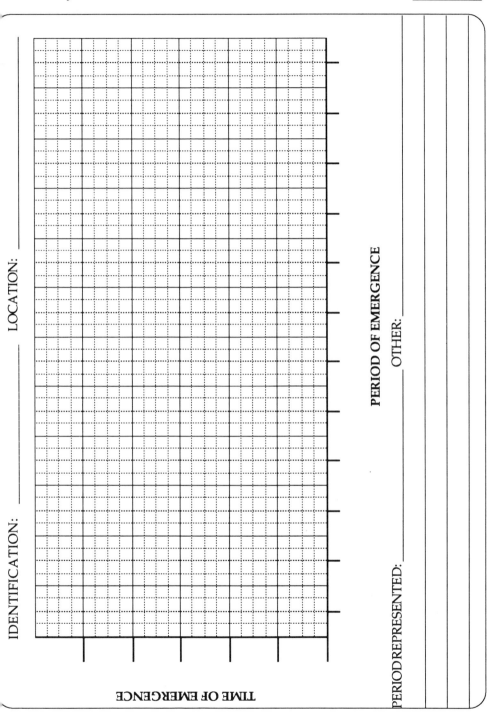

LOCATION: _____

IDENTIFICATION: _____

TIME OF EMERGENCE

PERIOD OF EMERGENCE

OTHER: _____

PERIOD REPRESENTED: _____

FISHING JOURNAL

HATCH CHAR

RECORD	DATE	TIME RANGE	TEMP RANGE		OTHER
			WATER	AIR	

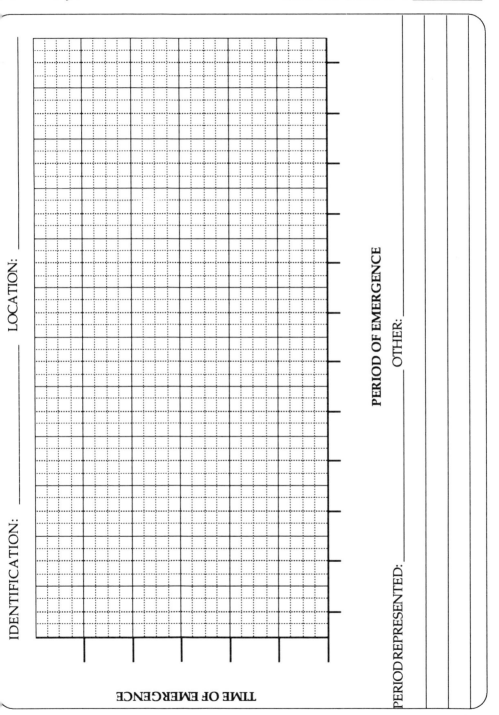

LOCATION: _____

IDENTIFICATION: _____

PERIOD OF EMERGENCE

OTHER: _____

PERIOD REPRESENTED: _____

TIME OF EMERGENCE

FISHING JOURNAL

RECORD	DATE	TIME RANGE	TEMP RANGE		OTHER
			WATER	AIR	

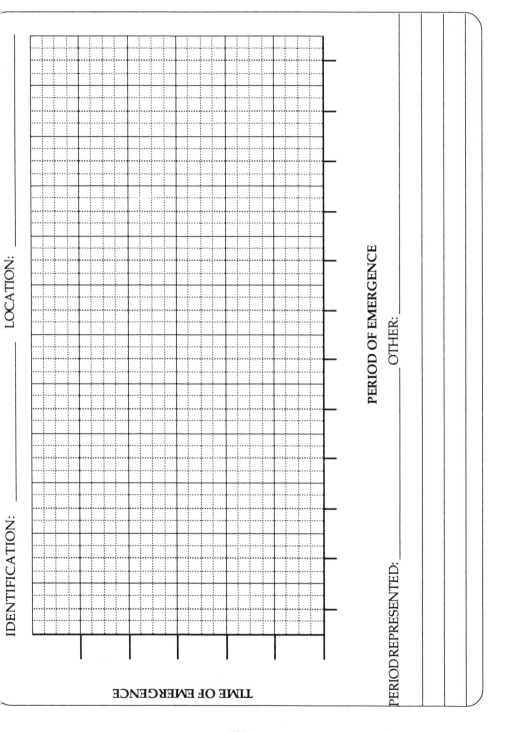

LOCATION: _____

IDENTIFICATION: _____

TIME OF EMERGENCE

PERIOD OF EMERGENCE

OTHER: _____

PERIOD REPRESENTED: _____

RECORD	DATE	TIME RANGE	TEMP RANGE		OTHER
			WATER	AIR	

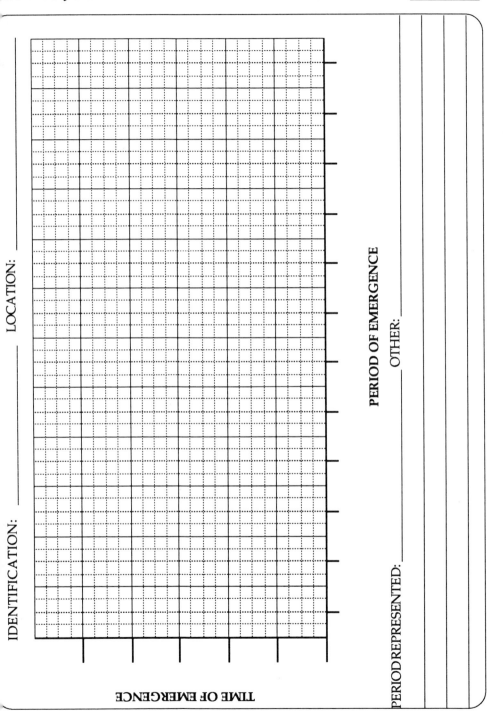

LOCATION: _____

IDENTIFICATION: _____

PERIOD OF EMERGENCE

OTHER: _____

PERIOD REPRESENTED: _____

TIME OF EMERGENCE

FISHING JOURNAL

HATCH CHAR

RECORD	DATE	TIME RANGE	TEMP RANGE		OTHER
			WATER	AIR	

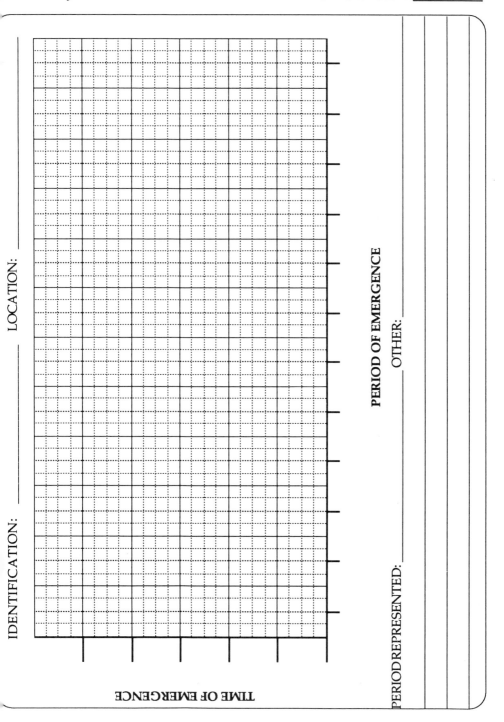

LOCATION: _____

IDENTIFICATION: _____

PERIOD OF EMERGENCE

OTHER: _____

PERIOD REPRESENTED: _____

TIME OF EMERGENCE

FISHING JOURNAL

HATCH CHAR

RECORD	DATE	TIME RANGE	TEMP RANGE		OTHER
			WATER	AIR	

PATTERN CHART# _____

INSECT INFO   IDENTIFICATION: _____

STAGE: _____ SAMPLES: _____DESCRIPTION:

HEAD _____

THORAX _____

ABDOMEN _____

IN WHOLE _____

HABITAT _____

NOTES _____

_____

STAGE: _____ SAMPLES: _____DESCRIPTION:

HEAD _____

THORAX _____

ABDOMEN _____

IN WHOLE _____

HABITAT _____

NOTES _____

_____

PATTERN INFO

NAME: _____ IMITATES: _____ MATERIALS:

HOOK _____ Nos. _____

_____ : _____

_____ : _____

_____ : _____

_____ : _____

_____ : _____

_____ : _____

_____ : _____

TYING NOTES: _____

_____

_____

_____

_____

NAME: _____ IMITATES: _____ MATERIALS:

HOOK _____ Nos. _____

_____ : _____

_____ : _____

_____ : _____

_____ : _____

_____ : _____

_____ : _____

_____ : _____

TYING NOTES: _____

_____

_____

_____

_____

INSECT INFO   IDENTIFICATION: _____

STAGE: _____ SAMPLES: _____ DESCRIPTION:

HEAD _____

THORAX _____

ABDOMEN _____

IN WHOLE _____

HABITAT _____

NOTES _____

_____

_____

STAGE: _____ SAMPLES: _____ DESCRIPTION:

HEAD _____

THORAX _____

ABDOMEN _____

IN WHOLE _____

HABITAT _____

NOTES _____

_____

_____

FISHING JOURNAL

PATTERN CHART

PATTERN INFO

NAME: _____ IMITATES: _____ MATERIALS:

HOOK _____ Nos. _____

_____ : _____

_____ : _____

_____ : _____

_____ : _____

_____ : _____

_____ : _____

_____ : _____

TYING NOTES: _____

_____

_____

_____

_____

_____

NAME: _____ IMITATES: _____ MATERIALS:

HOOK _____ Nos. _____

_____ : _____

_____ : _____

_____ : _____

_____ : _____

_____ : _____

_____ : _____

_____ : _____

TYING NOTES: _____

_____

_____

_____

_____

_____

INSECT INFO   IDENTIFICATION:_____

STAGE: _____ SAMPLES: _____DESCRIPTION:

HEAD _____

THORAX _____

ABDOMEN _____

IN WHOLE _____

HABITAT _____

NOTES _____

_____

_____

STAGE: _____ SAMPLES: _____DESCRIPTION:

HEAD _____

THORAX _____

ABDOMEN _____

IN WHOLE _____

HABITAT _____

NOTES _____

_____

_____

PATTERN INFO

NAME: _____ IMITATES: _____ MATERIALS:

HOOK _____ Nos. _____

_____ : _____

_____ : _____

_____ : _____

_____ : _____

_____ : _____

_____ : _____

_____ : _____

TYING NOTES: _____

_____

_____

_____

_____

_____

NAME: _____ IMITATES: _____ MATERIALS:

HOOK _____ Nos. _____

_____ : _____

_____ : _____

_____ : _____

_____ : _____

_____ : _____

_____ : _____

_____ : _____

TYING NOTES: _____

_____

_____

_____

_____

INSECT INFO　　　IDENTIFICATION:_____

STAGE: _____ SAMPLES: _____DESCRIPTION:

HEAD _____

THORAX _____

ABDOMEN _____

IN WHOLE _____

HABITAT _____

NOTES _____
_____
_____

STAGE: _____ SAMPLES: _____DESCRIPTION:

HEAD _____

THORAX _____

ABDOMEN _____

IN WHOLE _____

HABITAT _____

NOTES _____
_____
_____

FISHING JOURNAL

PATTERN CHAR

PATTERN INFO

NAME: _____ IMITATES: _____ MATERIALS:

HOOK _____ Nos. _____

_____ : _____

_____ : _____

_____ : _____

_____ : _____

_____ : _____

_____ : _____

_____ : _____

TYING NOTES: _____

_____

_____

_____

_____

_____

NAME: _____ IMITATES: _____ MATERIALS:

HOOK _____ Nos. _____

_____ : _____

_____ : _____

_____ : _____

_____ : _____

_____ : _____

_____ : _____

_____ : _____

TYING NOTES: _____

_____

_____

_____

_____

INSECT INFO   IDENTIFICATION:_____

STAGE: _____ SAMPLES: _____DESCRIPTION:

HEAD _____

THORAX _____

ABDOMEN _____

IN WHOLE _____

HABITAT _____

NOTES _____

_____

_____

STAGE: _____ SAMPLES: _____DESCRIPTION:

HEAD _____

THORAX _____

ABDOMEN _____

IN WHOLE _____

HABITAT _____

NOTES _____

_____

_____

PATTERN INFO

NAME: _____ IMITATES: _____ MATERIALS:

HOOK _____ Nos. _____

_____ : _____
_____ : _____
_____ : _____
_____ : _____
_____ : _____
_____ : _____
_____ : _____

TYING NOTES: _____
_____
_____
_____
_____
_____

NAME: _____ IMITATES: _____ MATERIALS:

HOOK _____ Nos. _____

_____ : _____
_____ : _____
_____ : _____
_____ : _____
_____ : _____
_____ : _____
_____ : _____

TYING NOTES: _____
_____
_____
_____
_____
_____

SHING JOURNAL   *PATTERN CHART#* _____

INSECT INFO   IDENTIFICATION:_____

STAGE: _____ SAMPLES: _____DESCRIPTION:

HEAD _____

THORAX _____

ABDOMEN _____

IN WHOLE _____

HABITAT _____

NOTES _____
_____
_____

STAGE: _____ SAMPLES: _____DESCRIPTION:

HEAD _____

THORAX _____

ABDOMEN _____

IN WHOLE _____

HABITAT _____

NOTES _____
_____
_____

PATTERN INFO

NAME: _____ IMITATES: _____ **MATERIALS:**

HOOK _____ Nos. _____

_____ : _____

_____ : _____

_____ : _____

_____ : _____

_____ : _____

_____ : _____

_____ : _____

TYING NOTES: _____

_____

_____

_____

_____

NAME: _____ IMITATES: _____ **MATERIALS:**

HOOK _____ Nos. _____

_____ : _____

_____ : _____

_____ : _____

_____ : _____

_____ : _____

_____ : _____

_____ : _____

TYING NOTES: _____

_____

_____

_____

_____

PATTERN CHART# _____

INSECT INFO   IDENTIFICATION:_____

STAGE: _____ SAMPLES: _____ DESCRIPTION:

HEAD _____

_____

THORAX _____

_____

ABDOMEN _____

_____

IN WHOLE _____

_____

HABITAT _____

_____

NOTES _____

_____

_____

STAGE: _____ SAMPLES: _____ DESCRIPTION:

HEAD _____

_____

THORAX _____

_____

ABDOMEN _____

_____

IN WHOLE _____

_____

HABITAT _____

_____

NOTES _____

_____

_____

FISHING JOURNAL   *PATTERN CHAR*

PATTERN INFO

NAME: _____ IMITATES: _____ MATERIALS:

HOOK _____ Nos. _____

_____ : _____
_____ : _____
_____ : _____
_____ : _____
_____ : _____
_____ : _____
_____ : _____

TYING NOTES: _____
_____
_____
_____
_____
_____

NAME: _____ IMITATES: _____ MATERIALS:

HOOK _____ Nos. _____

_____ : _____
_____ : _____
_____ : _____
_____ : _____
_____ : _____
_____ : _____
_____ : _____

TYING NOTES: _____
_____
_____
_____
_____
_____

PATTERN CHART# _____

INSECT INFO   IDENTIFICATION:_____

STAGE: _____ SAMPLES: _____DESCRIPTION:

HEAD _____

_____

THORAX _____

_____

ABDOMEN _____

_____

IN WHOLE _____

_____

HABITAT _____

_____

NOTES _____

_____

_____

STAGE: _____ SAMPLES: _____DESCRIPTION:

HEAD _____

_____

THORAX _____

_____

ABDOMEN _____

_____

IN WHOLE _____

_____

HABITAT _____

_____

NOTES _____

_____

_____

PATTERN INFO

NAME: _____ IMITATES: _____ **MATERIALS:**

HOOK _____ Nos. _____

_____ : _____
_____ : _____
_____ : _____
_____ : _____
_____ : _____
_____ : _____
_____ : _____

TYING NOTES: _____
_____
_____
_____
_____

NAME: _____ IMITATES: _____ **MATERIALS:**

HOOK _____ Nos. _____

_____ : _____
_____ : _____
_____ : _____
_____ : _____
_____ : _____
_____ : _____
_____ : _____

TYING NOTES: _____
_____
_____
_____
_____

INSECT INFO   IDENTIFICATION:_____

STAGE: _____ SAMPLES: _____DESCRIPTION:

HEAD _____

THORAX _____

ABDOMEN _____

IN WHOLE _____

HABITAT _____

NOTES _____

_____

_____

STAGE: _____ SAMPLES: _____DESCRIPTION:

HEAD _____

THORAX _____

ABDOMEN _____

IN WHOLE _____

HABITAT _____

NOTES _____

_____

_____

FISHING JOURNAL

PATTERN CHAR

PATTERN INFO

NAME: _____ IMITATES: _____ MATERIALS:

HOOK _____ Nos. _____

_____:_____

_____:_____

_____:_____

_____:_____

_____:_____

_____:_____

_____:_____

TYING NOTES: _____

_____

_____

_____

_____

NAME: _____ IMITATES: _____ MATERIALS:

HOOK _____ Nos. _____

_____:_____

_____:_____

_____:_____

_____:_____

_____:_____

_____:_____

_____:_____

TYING NOTES: _____

_____

_____

_____

_____

PATTERN CHART# _____

INSECT INFO   IDENTIFICATION: _____

STAGE: _____ SAMPLES: _____ **DESCRIPTION:**

HEAD _____

THORAX _____

ABDOMEN _____

IN WHOLE _____

HABITAT _____

NOTES _____
_____
_____

STAGE: _____ SAMPLES: _____ **DESCRIPTION:**

HEAD _____

THORAX _____

ABDOMEN _____

IN WHOLE _____

HABITAT _____

NOTES _____
_____
_____

FISHING JOURNAL

PATTERN INFO

NAME: _____ IMITATES: _____ MATERIALS:

HOOK _____ Nos. _____

_____: _____
_____: _____
_____: _____
_____: _____
_____: _____
_____: _____
_____: _____

TYING NOTES: _____
_____
_____
_____
_____
_____

NAME: _____ IMITATES: _____ MATERIALS:

HOOK _____ Nos. _____

_____: _____
_____: _____
_____: _____
_____: _____
_____: _____
_____: _____
_____: _____

TYING NOTES: _____
_____
_____
_____
_____
_____

EMERGENCE CALENDAR FOR _____

IDENTIFICATION	PERIOD OF EMERGENCE.												TIME OF ACTIVITY	COMMENTS	HATCH CHART REFS.	PATTERN CHART REFS.
	J	F	M	A	M	J	J	A	S	O	N	D				

FISHING JOURNAL   *HATCH CALENDAR # _____*

EMERGENCE CALENDAR FOR _____

IDENTIFICATION	PERIOD OF EMERGENCE.												TIME OF ACTIVITY	COMMENTS	HATCH CHART REFS.	PATTERN CHART REFS.
	J	F	M	A	M	J	J	A	S	O	N	D				

136

EMERGENCE CALENDAR FOR _____

IDENTIFICATION	PERIOD OF EMERGENCE. J F M A M J J A S O N D	TIME OF ACTIVITY	COMMENTS	HATCH CHART REFS.	PATTERN CHART REFS.

FISHING JOURNAL

HATCH CALENDAR # _____

EMERGENCE CALENDAR FOR _____

IDENTIFICATION	PERIOD OF EMERGENCE.												TIME OF ACTIVITY	COMMENTS	HATCH CHART REFS.	PATTERN CHART REFS.
	J	F	M	A	M	J	J	A	S	O	N	D				

EMERGENCE CALENDAR FOR _____

IDENTIFICATION	PERIOD OF EMERGENCE. J F M A M J J A S O N D	TIME OF ACTIVITY	COMMENTS	HATCH CHART REFS.	PATTERN CHART REFS.

EMERGENCE CALENDAR FOR _____

IDENTIFICATION	PERIOD OF EMERGENCE.												TIME OF ACTIVITY	COMMENTS	HATCH CHART REFS.	PATTERN CHART REFS.
	J	F	M	A	M	J	J	A	S	O	N	D				

EMERGENCE CALENDAR FOR

IDENTIFICATION	PERIOD OF EMERGENCE.												TIME OF ACTIVITY	COMMENTS	HATCH CHART REFS.	PATTERN CHART REFS.
	J	F	M	A	M	J	J	A	S	O	N	D				

EMERGENCE CALENDAR FOR _____

IDENTIFICATION	PERIOD OF EMERGENCE. J F M A M J J A S O N D	TIME OF ACTIVITY	COMMENTS	HATCH CHART REFS.	PATTERN CHART REFS.

EMERGENCE CALENDAR FOR _____

IDENTIFICATION	PERIOD OF EMERGENCE. J F M A M J J A S O N D	TIME OF ACTIVITY	COMMENTS	HATCH CHART REFS.	PATTERN CHART REFS.

FISHING JOURNAL

HATCH CALENDAR # _____

EMERGENCE CALENDAR FOR

IDENTIFICATION	PERIOD OF EMERGENCE.												TIME OF ACTIVITY	COMMENTS	HATCH CHART REFS.	PATTERN CHART REFS.
	J	F	M	A	M	J	J	A	S	O	N	D				

FISHING JOURNAL

EXTRA NOTES # _____

SHING JOURNAL   *EXTRA NOTES # _____*

EXTRA NOTES # _____

ABBREVIATIONS TABLE

This section is fairly self explanatory. You may find it helpful to use the abbreviations provided while making entries. They help save time and space, and will lend a degree of standardization which can be useful when making comparisons between entries.

DAILY RECORD

The Daily Record is the heart of the journal. It is where you record information, data, and thoughts about each fishing trip. It stands on its own as a record to be looked over in preparation for a trip or in trying to solve some of fishing's many mysteries. It is also the main source of information you will use in creating Hatch Charts, Calendars, and Pattern Charts for your favorite waters. Below is a description of components which may not be clear and some suggestions for recording information.

Daily Record # acts as a page number. Assuming it's the first trip in 1993, you might enter DR1-93. The **Location** section is pretty straight forward. **Section/ Access** records the area fished and how to get there; (e.g. Canyon, park at hatchery).

The **Weather** section is mostly self explanatory, and for the most part can be completed by checking, circling or slashing in the appropriate place. The **Air Temp.** can be recorded once, as a range (e.g. at the beginning and end of outing), or at a key event such as an emergence. **Sky, Wind** and **Precipitation** are observational, and the area for **Notes** allows more detail if wanted. Both **Barometer** and **Humidity** readings are available in most local papers, as is the lunar phase for those interested. It can also be worthwhile to note the time of recording and area where it was taken. A little scribble room is to be found in most of the boxes for those sorts of notes.

The **Water** section is also mostly check, circle, slash, and the suggestions for recording **Air Temp.** hold true for **Water Temp.**. The **Level** can be determined by looking at the flow in relation to the stream channel (e.g. comparing present level to the active channel, which is the area visibly influenced by water). Many larger rivers may have their level in feet or CFS reported in the local paper if you are interested in more exact data. The **Clarity** should be recorded based on your judgement and a word or two about the color/description of the water can be noted below the scale. The **Size** can be noted generally or in terms of stream order. The **Character** is intended to note features which characterize the system (e.g. closed canopy, high energy- rapids, plunge pools, little aquatic vegetation, etc.; or open, meandering w/ pools, glides and riffles, heavy weed beds, etc.). The character of a stream determines the aquatic insects which favor its water, and also plays a major role in what techniques will be effective for taking fish from its water. It can be very helpful to make comparisons to well known water when describing new water. The **Notes** area provides some room for such comparisons or other comments.

The **Notes & Sketches** section is just what it seems, a place for a map of a pool and the exact spot where you took a large steelhead, somewhere to jot things of interest or to describe an experience, or simply a place to write down the spill over from other sections. There is also additional note paper which can be linked to the entry (e.g. Extra Note # DR1-93) when more space is needed.

The **Time Line** section provides an easy place to record the time and sequence of events during the day. You can record the total time spent fishing, periods of hatches, when you recorded specific information or caught fish, etc. Its quick and can be especially useful in noting the chronological sequence of events (e.g. the time of key events in a hatch-nymphal activity, emergence, duns on water, etc.; or similarly the times of successful fishing techniques, nymphing, soft hackle on the swing, dead drift dry fly). When such records are compared over a period of a season or more, they can yield information about a hatch and its dynamics which are priceless to the angler.

The **Hatches** section provides a table where information about aquatic insects and their activity can be recorded. **Identification** to the order, family and sometimes genus level can be made at the stream, and more exact identifications can be made later if you collect samples. It's a good idea to note a sample or vial number along with your stream identification. This prevents confusion and allows you to better use information gained from your samples. The **Stage** section records the life stage of the insect observed, and the use of abbreviations here can be very helpful; (e.g. L.IN.NY., indicating a late instar nymph, etc.). The **Activity & Observations** is the place to note the activity of the insect and or observations; (e.g. H.IM.MF. or L.SI. on SU., etc.) **Water Type** records the area in which the insect is found (e.g. R., or P.), and the **Time** indicates when the activity was observed.

The **Fish** section provides a table where information about fish, fishing, and fishing techniques is recorded. This section is pretty straight forward and doesn't need much explanation. Again, abbreviations here can be useful, and you can break up observations according to individual fish, flies or however works for you. The use of # helps provide some flexibility in how you use this section.

In whole, the Daily Record is designed to be quick and easy, yet provide the flexibility to meet the needs of each angler. Over time you'll develop a style and technique of recording which works best for you and allows you to capture the information you want and need. Also, it may be helpful to organize the journal in several ways according to your needs. For instance, I use several journals depending on where I am fishing. I keep one for each of the waters I most often fish, and have one which acts as my travel journal for less frequently visited waters. This helps in organizing information about specific waters. The same end can be reached by using one journal, and later grouping entries according to location, type of hatch, etc.. There are a lot of possibilities, and I hope you have fun exploring them.

HATCH CHART

The Hatch Chart is a tool which allows you to combine information from a group of observations to create a chart which describes the period and time of emergence for an insect in a specific water or region. More simply, it lets you describe and analyze a specific hatch occurring at a specific area. There are a several ways this can be done, and different techniques which you can use to obtain results of different detail. Below I'll outline the basics of putting a chart together and will describe a couple of different ways to summarize observations.

Identification and **Location** can be used for a specific insect and location, or more broadly for a family of insects and a region, or a combination of the two. This allows you to make charts for most any situation. Again, the **Hatch Chart #** is simply a page number and the **Period Represented** indicates the time period for which data is summarized (e.g. 91-93 seasons). The **Time Of Emergence,** the Y-axis, indicates the time of day of activity; and the **Period Of Emergence,** X-axis, indicates the calendar days of activity. Up to six hours of activity can be denoted on the Y-axis and up to twelve months on the X-axis. The intervals of both the X and Y-axis can be grouped to allow greater detail over a shorter period of time, and in most cases a chart will only need to cover several months or less and a few hours of the day.

The back portion of the chart provides a table to summarize important information from the daily records used in creating a hatch chart. **Record** provides a place to indicate the page number of the entry for easy referencing back to the entries used, and the **Date** column indicates the date of the entry as well as period of emergence for that entry. The **Time Range** is where you note the time of day in which activity was observed, this is best entered as a range for the day (e.g. beginning to end), but can be entered as a single time if a range is not available. The **Temp. Range** for both **Water** and **Air** work in the same way, and are not directly used in creating a chart but are helpful in understanding the ways in which these two major factors influence a hatch.

Creating a hatch chart involves several steps. First, the data on the insect and location must be summarized, and it should be noted that the greater the amount of data used the better the results will be. Second, you must decide how you wish to plot the chart (time and period ranges to be used), and how you want to represent the information (simple range of activity, range of most activity, break the range up into types of activity-emergence/duns, etc.). Third, plot the data points on the graph and make your chart.

Unless you are a full time fishermen, there will be gaps in your data. The best solution to this problem is to get more data and fill in the blanks. As you collect information over a number of seasons you'll fill in some of these blanks, but you can also make a good guess by using adjacent points as a guide. If you have more than one entry for a particular day, take an average of the upper and lower limits of the ranges to get an average range. If you do not have a range for a given day, you can make a guess of what the range should be based on what the ranges on other days are.

Most of the information useful to the angler can be had by simply looking at the chart and its graphical representation of observations. Scientists use statistical techniques to analyze data and determine how significant the results are. You can do the same thing, in the rough, by analyzing the graph visually. Look for patterns, trends, times of greatest activity, etc. If a hatch on a given day doesn't seem to fit the pattern, look at the conditions during the day and how they differ from other days. There is a lot which can be learned by analyzing a hatch in such a way. The hatch chart illustrates trends and characteristics that typify a hatch, and the angler who creates and carefully analyzes a chart will be rewarded with a greater understanding of the dynamics of a hatch and the factors which influence it.

PATTERN CHART

The Pattern Chart serves two functions. It allows you to record information about insects, and about the patterns which imitate them. Because there is a lot of variation in local populations of aquatic insects, and most of us identify aquatic insects to the Genus or even Family level which allows for even more variation; this section can be very helpful in recording what is known about a local population and the patterns which work best for matching it. You can note the locality of the population in the **Notes** section or combine your knowledge of a number of populations to develop a pattern suitable for all waters having a population of the insect in question.

HATCH CALENDAR

The Hatch Calendar's primary function is to illustrate the period and time of emergence for all the hatches you are familiar with on a particular water or drainage, and to provide reference to the Hatch and Pattern Charts which are appropriate to the water. As such, it serves as a calendar of insect activity for a particular water and provides a guide to the time and type of fishing to be had during the year. Indeed, it ties all the information known about a specific water, its hatches, and effective patterns and techniques into one table. Below is a descriptions of the calendar components and how they can be used.

Emergence Calendar For indicates the specific water or drainage that is being illustrated. **Identification** refers to the insect described in the that row, and it makes sense to list the insects chronologically according to the time of year they are present. **Period Of Emergence** shows the time of year the insects are active. This can be done by listing an average start and end date in the appropriate months or by filling the area in to form a horizontal bar. **Time Of Activity** shows the time of day when the insects are active. This may be listed as a average range of time, start time, or whatever makes sense to you. Both the period of emergence and the time of activity can easily be determined from a hatch chart, but it is possible to figure them out without having one. The **Comments** column is pretty small, but will allow some room for making note of important information. Additionally, the **Hatch Chart Refs.** and **Pattern Chart Refs.** allow information shown on the calendar to be linked to more detailed information.

IN WHOLE

The description of the various components of the journal may be confusing, but it should make sense when you compare the descriptions to the examples (adapted from Pauls many years of notes on the Metolius River) shown in the following pages.

EXAMPLE DAILY RECORD   *DAILY RECORD # DR1-9*

LOCATION

Date: *6/14/92*   Stream/Lake: *Metolius River*

State *OR* County *Deschutes*   Section/Access *Canyon & lower*

section of gorge, parked at Wizzard Falls Hatchery & hiked up west bank

WEATHER

AIR TEMP	SKY		BAROMETER	Weather Notes:
100°–30° (10am *3pm)	*Mostly Clear, sparse clowds*		30 . 6	*Good w/ high drifting clowds, little wind, a lot of sun on water*

WIND	PRECIPITATION	
N / W–E / S — *Light*	[X] None ☐ Snow ☐ Drizzle ☐ Fog ☐ Showers ☐ Heavy Rain ☐ Thunderstorm	rising / falling / steady

HUMIDITY _30_ %

WATER

H₂0 TEMP	LEVEL	CLARITY	Water Notes:
80°–30° (10am *3pm)	High / Low	Clear ▸ Dirty — *Crystal Clear*	*Great as always*

rising / falling / steady

SIZE	CHARACTER
Med.	*Open spring creek w/ mod. gradient mostly R.P & G's*

NOTES & SKETCHES

Great day fishing plus hike up paid off with few other fishermen. The Drakes came off well and had great fun on dries with some nice native fish. Role cast was needed in most spots, so I think it might pay to use the 9 ft 6 weight to get more distance next time. Also, bring more flies as a lot were lost breaking of on fish and trees at the hog hole. Really tough casting, but really nice fish if you got a good drift. Took an exceptional fish from far side of this hole. It was taking dries aggressively from a really good converging current near the head of the pool. Tough drift, need to drop fly full 10 feet above and about 3 to right to get it over fish without any drag, and the fish are real picky + spooky.

Place cast here

Submerged Boulders

XAMPLE DAILY RECORD

TIME LINE   **HATCHES**   **FISH**

Time line: 6am 8am 10am 12am 2pm 4pm 6pm 8pm 10pm 12pm 2am 4am 6am

baetis coming off w/ peak activity towards end

Nice Rainbow

Drakes began about 2 & were still going when I left at 3

HATCHES

IDENTIFICATION	STAGE	ACTIVITY & OBSERVATIONS	WATER TYPE	TIME
Baetis Sp. V#1	Sl.	S. Sl's drifting on SU. + quickly airborn	R, G, & P's	10/11
Perlidae (A.c.?) V#2	2 LINNY,	1min drift sample from B. of H.R.	R.	11:30
Perlidae (A.c.?)	AD.	LI #'s airborn + more on vegetation	On veg. & in air	N/A
Ephemerella (E.g.?) V#3	1 LINNY,	Same sample as stones		
Ephemerella (E.g.?) V#4	Sl.	M. #'s drifting on SU. of P.	P. w/ emerg.	
		w/ long drift before flight	in above R.?	2/3pm

FISH

SPECIES	PATTERN	OBSERVATIONS & METHODS	WATER TYPE	SIZE	TIME	#
OM.	#18 baetis compara	Down & accross dead drift	R, G, & P's	11 to 14"	10/11	4
ST.	#18 baetis compara	Down & accross dead drift	G.	15"	10:30	1
OM.	#8 Metolius stone &	Short line nymph w/ dropper	R. & FA.P.	10 to 16	11:30	7
	#10 drake NY.dropper				to 1	
OM.	#12 drake compara	Up & accross dead drift	P.	12 to 15	1/3	3
	#12 paradrake			19.5"	2:30	1

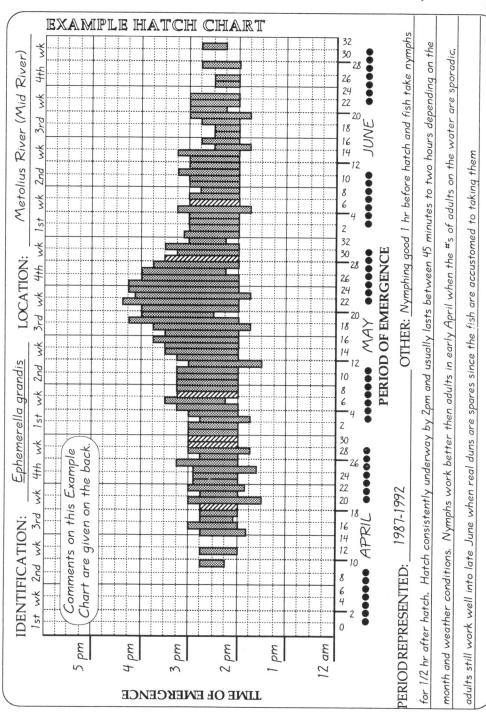

| RECORD | DATE | TIME RANGE | TEMP RANGE | | OTHER |
			WATER	AIR	
DR1-92	6/14/92	2-3pm ->?	54-56	64-76	clear and sunny
DR2-92	6/15/92	1:45-2:30pm	55	62-65	overcast and cool
DR3-92	6/23/92	2-3pm	55-57	70-82	sunny, high clowds
DR4-91	5/22/91	2-4:10pm	54-56	65-74	sunny and clear
ETC.					
ETC.					

Example Comments: Notice that the ▨ bars indicate gaps in the data which were filled using estimates based on adjoining days. Also, notice how the chart illustrates that the most common time of activity (for the entire period of the hatch) is between 2 and 3pm. Additionally, it shows how the duration (total time of activity) of the hatch increases from about the 4th week in April until it peaks in the last week of May. It then decreases until it levels off in early June. If you were able to look at the notes used in creating this chart you would also find that this period also represents the period of heaviest Drake hatches.

This chart also shows that the start time for the hatch is practically constant through out the entire period of emergence. This is typical of spring creeks like the Metolius which have virtually constant water temperatures and level through out the season. In free stone creeks and rivers which experience more pronounced water fluctuations and tend to experience significant water temperature changes (e.g. warming from spring into summer), the chart can show trends in the time of activity as insects adjust the timing of their activity to maintain the same environmental conditions. For instance, the start time may progressively shift to an earlier or later time in response to the changing daily temperature regime of the stream

INSECT INFO	IDENTIFICATION:	*Ephemerella grandis*

STAGE: _____*Late instar nymph*_____ SAMPLES: *M. R. 6/14/92 V#3*DESCRIPTION

HEAD _*Broad, roughly same width as thorax. Dark mottled olive brown, short*_
antenna, total length of head 3/32 inch.

THORAX _Broad, dark mottled olive brownish with more olivish sternum, 1/4"_
total length. Wing cases are darker shade of sternum color, 3/16"

ABDOMEN _Color same as thorax w/ dark markings on each tergum. 3 amber_
tails with dark brown mottling (3/8"). Gills grayish olive.

IN WHOLE _Size ave. 3/4" w/ body shape somewhat flattened and blockish lookin_
Color is mottled olive and brown w/dark striations on backside and legs.

HABITAT _Distributed widely, but seeming to prefer heavy riffles to rapids,_
seeking pockets of slack water within these habitats

NOTES _Reference info: Hatches II (Caucci & Nastastasi, 1985), pp. 104-110;_
Matching the Hatch (Schwiebert, 1955), pp. 105-106; Nymphs (Schwiebert,
1973), pp. 293-310; Western Hatches (Hafele & Hughes, 1981), pp. 57-64.

STAGE: _____*Dun*_____ SAMPLES: *M. R. 6/14/92 V#4*DESCRIPTION:

HEAD _Small, greenish brown in color with prominent dark greyish/blak_
eyes.

THORAX _Green brown in color with slate grey wings w/ height of 3/8 to 1/2"._
Legs are moderately thin, & same color as body.

ABDOMEN _Greenish brown in color with light banding at rear of each seg-_
ment, & lighter color on underside. 3 mottled dark gray tails about 3/8" long.

IN WHOLE _Size ave. 5/8" with fairly stout body. The color ranges from bright_
greenish brown to more subtle greenish brown. Wings & tails very prominent

HABITAT _Seem to prefer emerging in gentle water near nymph habitat. Duns_
concetrated directly below these area, but widely distributed on river.

NOTES _Same refs as above, with best info in Hatches II and Western_
Hatches. Some good photos in both of these.

PATTERN INFO

NAME: _W. Green Drake Nymph_ IMITATES: _Green Drake Nymph_ MATERIALS:

HOOK _Mustad 9671 (2X long)_ Nos. _8 or 10_

Thread   : _6/0 Olive_

Tails   : _3 Dark barred woodduck barbules_

Dubbing   : _4/5 dark brown hares mask and 1/5 olive mask blended in_

Wing Pads   : _Dark mottled turkey feather_

Legs   : _Dark brown partridge_

Weight   : _Several twists of lead matching shank diameter_

     :

TYING NOTES: _Tye in lead where thorax will be, then dub very small tuft at end of hook and tie in tails using tuft to seperate them. Dub body and thorax, then tie in partridge below shank so it slanks back towards point of hook. Tie on wing case so that it covers half of body, wrap until covered and head is formed, whip finish._

EXAMPLE PATTERN CHART

NAME: _Compara-Dun Drake_ IMITATES: _Green Drake dun_ MATERIALS:

HOOK _Mustad 94833 (3X fine)_ Nos. _8 to 12_

Thread   : _6/0 Olive_

Tails   : _3 Dark grey microfibules_

Dubbing   : _Dark brownish olive synthetic_

Wings   : _Dark grey deer hair_

     :

     :

     :

TYING NOTES: _Tye in wing (slightly forward of half way point) first, and be sure to post it well. Tie in tails using small tuft of dubbing to split. Dub body forward and whip finish. Pages 301 to 313 of Hatches II for detailed tying instructions_

EXAMPLE HATCH CALENDAR

EMERGENCE CALENDAR FOR _Metolius River_

IDENTIFICATION	PERIOD OF EMERGENCE (J F M A M J J A S O N D)	TIME OF ACTIVITY	COMMENTS	HATCH CHART REFS.	PATTERN CHART REFS.
Baetis		All Day	Mid Day Best		
Little Winter Stone		Mid Day	Mid Day Best		
October Caddis		Late Morning to dusk			
Pale Morning Dun		Mid Morning to Mid Afternoon			
Caddis (various sp.)		Late Morning to dusk		HC1-92	PC1-92
Green Drake		Mid Day	Spinners Mid Morning		
Ants		All Day	Occurs after first 10 days above 70° in spring		
Golden Stonefly		All Day	Night Emergence		
Spruce Moth		Varried			
Grasshopper's		Mid Morning to Late Afternoon			
Brown Caddis		Late Morning to Dusk			
Spotted Sedge		Late Morning to Dusk			
Autumn Rithrogenia		Early Afternoon			
Autumn Green Drake		Mid Afternoon			
Small Dark Quills		Mid Morning to Mid Afternoon			
Little Green Stone		Late Morning to Late Afternoon			
Little Yellow Stones		Late Morning to Late Afternoon			
Diptera (various sp)					